50 LITTLE GIFTS

EASY
Patchwork
Projects to
Give or Swap

MW00800764

COMPILED BY SUSANNE WOODS

Published in 2018 by Lucky Spool Media, LLC
www.luckyspool.com
info@luckyspool.com

Text © The Individual Designers
Editor: Susanne Woods
Designer: Rae Ann Spitzenberger
Illustrator: Courtney Kyle
Photographer: Page + Pixel
(unless otherwise noted)

Photographs on page 28 © Anna Graham, page
52 ©Vanessa Hewell, pages 62 & 72 © Holly
DeGroot, page 64 © Paula Pepin, page 76 ©
Denyse Schmidt, page 83 © Susanne Woods
and pages 125 & 128 © Nicole Young

9 8 7 6 5 4 3 2 1
First Edition
Printed in China

Library of Congress Cataloging-in-
Publication Data available upon request
ISBN 978-1-940655-33-8
LSID0037

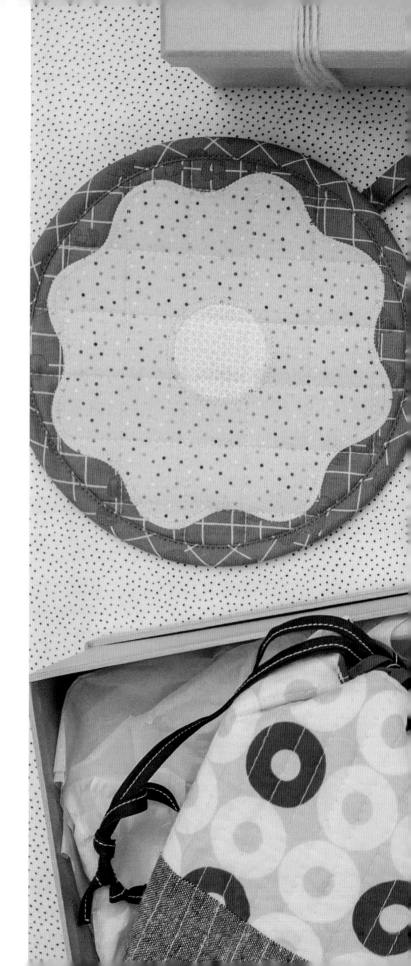

CONTENTS

WELCOME TO 50 LITTLE GIFTS!

If you are anything like me, you love to create adorable, fast, fun and useful gifts for friends and family. But you get overwhelmed sifting through hundreds of online tutorials to find just what you are looking for, or get frustrated trying to remember where you saw that perfect project you want to make *now*. That search (and I know you've done it too!) takes the 'fast' out of the equation pretty quickly, with the 'fun' closely heading out the door after it.

Never more! I've invited some talented designers to contribute beautiful small projects with the goal of compiling all of your favorites and basics into one place. If you want thoughtful little sewing projects, then this is the book you have been waiting for.

I love editing compilation books because you get the best from everyone! Some projects I've included are popular tried-and-true tutorials, and some are brand new, made just for this book. *50 Little Gifts* will be the book you grab each and every time you want to make that perfect small handmade gift.

Though a lot of these projects are perfect for sewing with beginners, I assume that you are a sewing enthusiast, with a decent stash of fabrics and scraps, who knows their way around a sewing machine (including how and when to use your zipper foot), how close to the edge you like your edgestitching and the difference between pressing and ironing. That's you, right?

To prevent repetition in each project, be aware that **all of the seam allowances are the standard ¼"** unless otherwise noted, and many of the projects don't include exact fabric requirements because they are scrappy or improvisational.

There is a lot of room for customization—adding decorative stitches, fussy cutting panels, incorporating leather or appliqué. So don't just stop at our basic instructions. Find your favorites, jazz them up using some of your favorite techniques and materials, and get gifting!

SUSANNE

LITTLE TUTORIAL:
BASIC EMBROIDERY STITCHES

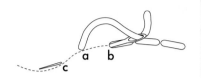

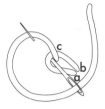

CROSS STITCH

Bring the needle up at (a) and down at (b). Bring the needle back up at (c). Continue for the desired number of stitches. Bring the needle up at (d), down at (e) and back up at (f) continuing to cross all of the (a/b) stitches.

BACKSTITCH

Bring the needle up at (a), go down at (b) very near the previous stitch, and come back up at (c), filling in the line desired. Try to keep the length of the stitches consistent.

CHAIN STITCH

Make a small backstitch from (a) to (b) leaving a small loop of thread. Bring the needle up at (c) and slip it under the loop of the backstitch. Take the needle down very close to (c). Continue by going under the loop formed in each previous chain stitch.

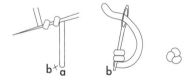

BLANKET STITCH

Come up at (a), go down at (b), leaving a loop of thread. Come up again at (c) with the needle on the inside of the loop of thread, catching it to make a backward L shape.

RUNNING STITCH

A popular basic stitch frequently used in Sashiko and visible mending. Bring needle up at (a), go down at (b), and come back up at (c) filling the line desired. Try to keep the length of the stitches consistent.

FRENCH KNOT

Bring the needle up at (a). wind the thread twice around the needle. Keeping the tension consistent in the thread, go down at (b) very close to (a) and pull the needle through the fabric to secure the knot.

FOR OPTIONAL APPLIQUÉ

1. Transfer your selected letter or number templates onto the paper side of freezer paper.

2. Position the shiny side of the freezer paper on the wrong side of the wool or fabric and press.

3. Cut out the appliqué shapes using the transferred template lines as a guide and remove the freezer paper.

4. Organize the trimmed shapes onto the right side of the project and baste in place.

5. Finish by sewing around the appliqué using a backstitch, blanket stitch (see above) or other decorative stitch. Use Perle cotton or embroidery floss for a chunkier look or an all-purpose thread if you don't want your stitches to show.

BY SUSANNE WOODS

Finished Size: 10" x 6"

MATERIALS

Exterior: 1 Fat Quarter

Lining: 1 Fat Quarter

Signature fabric: 5" Scrap

Fusible Interfacing: ¼ yard

Fusible tape or fabric glue

10" zipper

Zipper foot

CUTTING

From the Exterior Fabric, cut:
(1) 11" x 7" rectangle (back panel)
(1) 11" x 2½" strip
(1) 11" x 1½" strip
(2) 4" x 1½" rectangles
(2) 4" squares
(2) 1½" x 4" rectangles (optional zipper Tabs)

From the Lining Fabric and Interfacing, cut:
(2) 11" x 7" rectangles

From the Signature Scrap, cut:
(1) 4" x 2" rectangle

TIP: *If you'd like to add embroidery to your rectangle, do this before cutting the Signature Scrap rectangle.*

ASSEMBLING THE EXTERIOR PANELS

1. Sew a 1½" x 4" Exterior rectangle to either long side of the 2" x 4" Signature Scrap rectangle and press.

2. Sew a 4" Exterior square to either side of the pieced unit from Step 1 and press.

3. Sew the 1½" x 11" Background fabric strip to the bottom and the 2½" x 11" Background fabric strip to the top of the assembled unit from Step 2. This is now the Front Exterior Panel.

SIGNATURE BASIC BAG

This project is first because you will be referring to this basic bag assembly for any of the other zipper bags in the book. There are many optional extras you can include on your basic bag including adding zipper tabs, attaching a hang tag or handle, boxing the corners, or even omitting the patchwork front altogether and using (2) 11" x 7" rectangles for the Exterior for an even speedier finish!

I wanted to create an opportunity for customizing by adding a 'signature' panel in the middle of this basic bag. For mine, I riffed off the nautical theme of my fabric by adding embroidered initials using a Perle cotton. For your gift, consider adding in a favorite fussy cut phrase or incorporate a small piece of novelty fabric that befits the occasion of your handmade gift. Is this bag a little too big? No problem! Simply adjust your Exterior and Lining rectangles to the size you need, be sure your zipper is the correct size, and you're on your way!

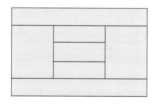

4. Fuse the Interfacing to the wrong side of both the Front and Back Exterior Panels.

ATTACHING THE OPTIONAL ZIPPER TABS

NOTE: If omitting the Tabs, the zipper must be the same length as the Exterior Panel, in this case 11".

1. Fold the (2) 1½" x 4" rectangles for the Tabs in half, short ends together, and with the wrong sides together. Press. Set aside.

2. Center the Front Exterior Panel along the zipper tape, without overlapping the pieces. Position the fusible tape on the zipper, 1" from each side edge of the Front Exterior Panel's edges and perpendicular to the zipper.

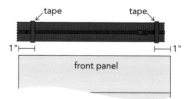

3. Center the folded Tabs from Step 1 on the zipper ends, with the folded edge facing toward the zipper. Press Tabs to the Tape to secure in place.

4. Sew both Tabs onto the zipper tape as close to the folded edges as possible. Trim away the excess zipper from under the Tabs leaving at least a ⅛" seam allowance.

ATTACHING THE ZIPPER

1. With the zipper face up, place fusible tape or fabric glue on the bottom edge of your zipper tape.

tape

2. Position the Front Exterior Panel (right side up), center the zipper (facing down with the zipper pull on the left side), and a Lining panel (wrong side up).

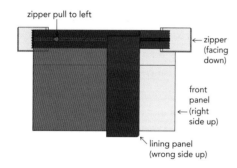

zipper pull to left

← zipper (facing down)

front panel ← (right side up)

↖ lining panel (wrong side up)

3. Press along the edge of the zipper so that the fusible tape adheres to the Front Exterior Panel. Using the zipper foot attachment on your machine, sew along the zipper tape.

> **TIP:** If using Tabs, you will be stitching over the folded Tabs as well, but will have some extra fabric that will be trimmed later. Align the Exterior and Lining Panels, not the Tabs.

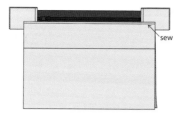

sew

4. Position the Front Exterior Panel and Lining wrong sides together. Press away from the zipper. Edgestitch along the right side of the Front Exterior Panel, close to the fold.

5. Repeat Steps 2-4 for the opposite side.

> **TIP:** If adding a hang tag or a handle, baste this to one edge of the Front Exterior Panel now, using a ⅛" seam allowance.

SEWING THE BAG

1. Switch back to a ¼" foot. Unzip the zipper halfway. Position both Exterior Panels on one side of the zipper and the Lining Panels are on the other, both with their right sides together. Starting in the middle of the long side of the Lining, sew around the perimeter, leaving a 3" opening for turning the bag.

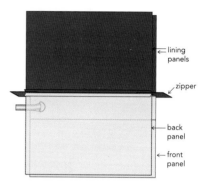

← lining panels

↙ zipper

← back panel

← front panel

2. Box the corners using the Pinch & Cut method if desired (see opposite).

3. Trim away the excess fabric from the Zipper Tabs.

FINISHING

1. Turn the bag right side out and push the corners out using a chopstick or similar blunt object. Hand or machine sew the opening closed. Push the Lining inside the Exterior. Press.

2. Carefully push out the corners near the zipper. On the inside of the bag, hand stitch a few tacking stitches to secure the Lining to the Exterior. This will help retain the bag's shape.

3. Attach an optional Zipper Pull if desired (see facing page).

LITTLE TUTORIAL:
CREATING BOXED CORNERS TWO WAYS

This book includes projects that have boxed corners. You can achieve these by using one of the two methods listed below (or leave the corners un-boxed if you prefer).

PINCH & CUT METHOD

1. With the bag still wrong side out, pinch one corner of the Lining Panel and position the bag sideways so the side seam of the Lining is centered on the bottom seam, forming a point. Press. Measure 1" down from the corner seam and mark a line perpendicular to the seam with a water soluble marker.

2. Sew on the marked line. Using an acrylic ruler with a ¼" line, trim the excess fabric, leaving a ¼" seam allowance.

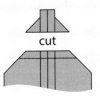

3. Repeat on the other corner of the Lining and the two corners of the Exterior Panels.

NOTCHED CORNER METHOD

1. To box the corners using the Notched Corner Method, your project will include instructions for cutting the appropriately sized square from two bottom corners on both the Exterior and the Lining Panels. Sew along the side seams and the bottom seam leaving the notched corners unsewn.

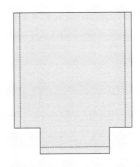

2. With the bag still wrong side out, pinch the side and the bottom together on one corner of the Lining. Align the sewn sides, nest the seams and pin in place.

3. Stitch across the opening.

4. Repeat Steps 2-3 for the other Lining corner and for both corners of the Exterior Panel.

NO BOXING METHOD

1. If you want to create a super-simple and super-speedy pouch, omit boxing the corners entirely.

2. To do this, simply stitch around the perimeter of the bag, leaving a 3" gap in the Lining for turning.

3. Clip the corners to reduce the bulk being careful not to cut through your stitching and finish the bag per the instructions.

ATTACHING THE OPTIONAL ZIPPER PULL TASSEL

1. Cut a 3" length of leather into ⅛" strips, or cut (2) 3" lengths of ⅛" ribbon.

2. Thread a 6" length of string through the hole in the zipper pull.

3. Place the leather/ribbon strips in the ribbon loop.

4. Gently tug the leather/ribbon through the hole in the zipper pull using the string.

5. Remove the string and thread the ends of the leather/ribbon through the loop on the right side of the pull. Tug the ends of the leather/ribbon until they are tight against the zipper pull.

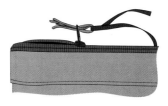

TRIANGULAR LOG CABIN PINCUSHION

This pincushion features a twist on a traditional log cabin block. While most log cabin blocks have a square or rectangular center, this project is built around a triangular center, which results in a unique finished shape. The pincushion is perfect for using up long skinny strips from your stash. It may look complicated, but it is built from the center outward just like a traditional log cabin block. I used my backing fabric choice as a starting point for my pincushion's color scheme, working with a range of jewel tones. Because the strips will be ¾" wide in the finished pincushion, simple small-scale prints work best for this project. Make the most of your time by making a few cushions assembly-line-style and you'll never be caught without a gift for your crafty friends. It is a great addition to any pincushion collection.

BY JENI BAKER

Finished Size: 6" per side

MATERIALS
At least (6) 4"-8" lengths of 1¼" wide fabric Strips
Center Fabric: 2" square
Backing Fabric: 7" square
Acrylic ruler
Pincushion filling
Water soluble marker

ASSEMBLING THE LOG CABIN TOP

1. Using an acrylic ruler and pencil, mark ⅞" away from each edge along the top edge of the 2" Center square. Draw a line connecting a ⅞" mark to the opposite corner. Repeat with the remaining mark. Cut along the two drawn lines to create the Center triangle.

2. Position the Center triangle and a Strip right sides together, with the triangle approximately 1" away from the end of the Strip. Sew the Center triangle to the Strip. Press the seam open.

3. Align an acrylic ruler along the edge of the Center triangle and trim away the excess Strip fabric. Repeat for the other edge.

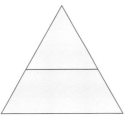

4. Rotate the assembled unit from Step 3 and position it right sides together on the next Strip, about 1" away from one end. Sew together and press the seam open.

5. Trim away the excess Strip on both edges as you did in Step 3.

6. Repeat Steps 4-5 until all 6 Strips have been attached to the Center triangle.

ASSEMBLING THE PINCUSHION

1. Use the pieced Top as a template to cut the back. Place the Top onto the Backing square, right sides together. Using a water soluble marker, trace around the triangle onto the square. Cut along the drawn lines.

2. With the Top and Backing still right sides together, pin and sew around all three edges, leaving a 2" opening on one edge for turning. Backstitch a few extra times at the start and finish.

3. Carefully clip the corners close to the seam allowance. Turn your pincushion right side out through the opening from Step 2, pushing out the corners gently with a chopstick or similar blunt object.

4. Stuff the pincushion with filling and hand-stitch the opening closed.

> **FILLING TIP:** Consider using crushed walnut shells (commonly sold as lizard litter in pet stores) as filling. It gives the pincushion a more substantial feel, allowing it to work double-duty as a pattern weight too!

BY CRYSTAL JOHNSEN

Finished Size: 1½" x 6"

MATERIALS
Home-Dec Fabric:
(2) 2" x 9" rectangles
(1) 2" D-ring

TIP: *If you want to use quilting cotton instead of a Home-Dec weight, just add a layer of heavy weight fusible interfacing to the wrong side of both rectangles.*

LIP BALM CARRIER

Need to make a bunch of cute, thrifty gifts in a hurry? This Carrier costs pennies in materials, uses up those fabrics in your scrap bin and takes fewer than five minutes to make. They make great teacher, party, secret Santa gifts and more!

Going on a family vacation? Pair this with the Water Bottle Carrier (see page 46) and make one to hold lip balm and the other to hold a tube of sunblock to be sure everyone is hydrated and protected. These carriers can be customized with school colors, fun holiday and novelty themes and you can even match your fabrics with the colorful lip balm packaging itself. It's a quick little way to show appreciation without breaking the bank.

1. Position the 2 rectangles right sides together. Sew along three edges, leaving one short edge open. Clip all the corners.

2. Turn the carrier right side out and gently push out the corners using a chopstick or similar blunt object. Press well, being sure to tuck in the seam allowance of the un-sewn end, but not sewing it closed yet.

3. Fold up the short closed edge by about 2½". Press well.

4. Sewing as close to the edge as you feel comfortable, sew along the sides and bottom edge of the folded end.

5. Fold the un-sewn short edge end over to the front by 1" and press, being sure the seam allowances and raw edges are nicely tucked into the opening. Position the D-ring in place with the straight edge in the fold. Sew through all of the layers along the short edge, closing the opening from Step 1.

BY PENNY LAYMAN

Finished Size: 51" x 11"

MATERIALS

Exterior: 1½ yards

Lining: 1½ yards Flannel

(3) 1" buttons

Water soluble marker

(1) 10" length of ⅛" wide cording

These instructions are for creating a 51" long scarf. If you would like to make a shorter or longer scarf, decrease or increase the 52" cut length to achieve your desired length.

All seam allowances are ⅜".

CUTTING

From the Exterior and Lining Fabrics, cut:

(1) 52" X 11½" rectangle

From the cording, cut:

(3) 2⅝" lengths

LITTLE TUTORIAL: MAKING CORDING

To make your own ⅛" wide cording, start with a ½" wide strip of fabric and use a bias tape maker to create ¼" single fold bias tape. Fold the ¼" tape in half and sew the folded edges together to yield ⅛" wide cording. You may need to move the needle position to one side as you are sewing, to ensure that the feed dogs will feed the narrow fabric through.

MODIFIED INFINITY SCARF

My scarf pattern was born out of a desire to shorten the length of the standard 60" infinity scarf so it isn't as bulky and doesn't hang so low. I added a cording-and-button closure to give an alternative to pulling it on over my head, since I usually put my scarves on as I'm walking out the door after I've already done my hair. I also use flannel as the lining for an extra-cozy feel. This scarf is a super-simple make, and will take only 30 minutes to put together. While my instructions are for making a single scarf, you can create three from the yardage listed.

ASSEMBLING THE SCARF

1. With the right sides together, sew the Lining and Exterior rectangles along one of the 52" sides and press the seam open.

2. With the fabrics still pressed open, sew a gathering stitch along the two short ends of the assembled unit from Step 1. Do this by adjusting the stitch length on your machine as long as possible. Next, sew ⅛" from the raw edge, then sew a second parallel line of stitching ¼" from the edge.

NOTE: *Do **not** secure the gathering stitches on either end.*

3. Pull the top threads on one side of your gathering stitches to gather the scarf edge so it measures 12" wide. Make sure that the Lining and Exterior fabrics are evenly gathered, so each one is 6" wide. Repeat for the other short edge.

4. Edgestitch ¼" from each edge to secure the gathers in place.

5. Fold the three lengths of cording in half and pin them along one short edge of the

wrong side of the Exterior at 1¾", 3" and 4¾" away from the long top edge. Align the raw edges so the loops are positioned inwards. Stitch ¼" from the edge, basting the loops in place.

6. Fold the scarf in half, right sides together along the first long seam you sewed in Step 1. Pin and sew the three edges together, leaving a 3" opening along the remaining long edge for turning.

7. Turn the scarf right side out, tuck in the seam allowances of the opening. Press and either hand sew or machine topstitch the opening closed.

8. Evenly mark and attach the buttons onto the short gathered edge that doesn't have the cording loops, each about 1½" away from the gathered edge.

RIC RAC CLUTCH

This adorable little clutch is one of my favorite go-to gifts. It is so simple to make that you can make a couple of them in just a few hours! This is perfect for gifting to teachers, bridesmaids, best friends ... or even to keep all for yourself! With a simple change of fabric you can have a sweet little everyday bag to go with jeans or an elegant clutch perfect for a fancy night out. This purse is a lightweight, compact and stylish way to take your essentials with you, wherever you go.

Looking to add some character to another project in the book? Stitch up one of my flowers to add a feminine touch to anything from Kristin's Mason Jar Cozy (see page 84) to Penny's Infinity Scarf (see page 16).

5

BY JENNIFER LADD

....

Finished Size: 9" x 4¾"

MATERIALS

Exterior: ⅓ yard

Lining: ⅓ yard

(1) 7" Yellow Fabric square
for the petals

(1) 2" White scrap of Felt for
the flower center (optional)

(1) 2" Gold scrap of Felt for
the flower backing

(1) 30" length of ½" wide ric rac

(1) 1" button

Medium weight fusible
Interfacing: 1 yard

Magnetic snap

Water soluble marker

CUTTING AND
PREPARATION

1. Using the Purse Panel pattern
(see page 21), cut 1 from the
Exterior and Lining Fabrics, and
2 from the Fusible Interfacing.
Transfer the markings onto the
right sides of the panels using a
water soluble marker.

2. Fuse the Interfacing onto the
wrong side of each cut panel.

3. Photocopy and cut out the
Flower Petal (see page 21).

ATTACHING THE RIC RAC

1. Position the Exterior Panel
right side up on a work surface.
Use pins to mark the starting
points for the ric rac. Using a
long basting stitch and without
backstitching, sew a line from
pin-to-pin, using a ⅝" seam
allowance. This line will be the
guide for applying the ric rac.

2. Carefully pin the ric rac to the
right side of the Exterior Panel
so that the bottom bumps of
the ric rac come just below the
basting line. When assembling
the purse, only the bumps of the
ric rac will be visible, so that
is the only part that should be
below the basting line.

> **NOTE:** *It is important to spend
> some extra time ensuring that
> the ric rac is attached as evenly
> as possible so that it looks
> consistent on the finished bag.
> Also, be careful cutting the
> ends of the ric rac. Be certain
> the cut ends face toward the
> raw edges so that they will be
> secured in the seam allowance.
> You do not want those ugly
> raw edges showing up in your
> finished bag!*

3. Still using a basting stitch and
a ½" seam allowance, sew the ric
rac into place. Set aside.

ASSEMBLING THE FLOWER

1. Fold the Petal fabric in half,
right sides together. Cut 6 Petal
pairs using the Flower Petal
pattern. Pin each pair together
right sides facing so that they
don't shift while sewing.

2. Stitch around the curved edge
of the 6 Petal pairs, leaving the
bottom open. Backstitch at both
ends of the seam.

3. Trim the seam allowance to
⅛" to reduce the bulk and clip
the edges to help with turning.

4. Turn each Petal right side out
and press.

5. Using a long basting stitch
and a ¼" seam allowance, sew
the turned Petals along their
bottom edge producing a long
line of the 6 Petals. Leave thread
tails at the end for gathering.
Do **not** trim these threads or
backstitch at the beginning
or end of your sewing.

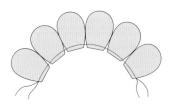

6. Take hold of the top thread on
one side of the attached Petal
arc (leaving the bottom thread
alone) and pull gently while
slowly pushing the fabric in the
opposite direction. The Petals
will begin to gather at the
bottom and you will see the
flower form. Work from both
sides so that it is easier to keep
the gathers even. Be sure to
work slowly and carefully ... if
the thread breaks, you will have
to start over again.

7. Using the square of Gold Felt, position the Petals into a circle and pin the flower to the Felt. Sew a circle along the bottom edge of the Petals through all of the layers using a 1/8" seam allowance. Trim around the excess Felt in the shape of a circle to create a neat finish.

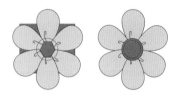

8. Pin the flower in place on the right side of the Exterior Panel with the Gold Felt circle facing down and using the transferred mark from the pattern for reference. Sew a circle around the raw edges of the Petals to attach the flower to the Exterior Panel.

9. If your button isn't large enough to cover the Gold circle, free-form cut a flower shape from the White Felt. Arrange this over the circle from Step 8. Position the button on top of the White Felt and hand stitch through all layers to attach. If your button is large enough, simply omit the white flower.

ATTACHING THE SNAP

Using the placement guide on the pattern as a reference, and following the manufacturer's instructions, attach one side of the magnetic snap to the right side of the Exterior Panel and the other side to the right side of the Lining Panel. Back each on the wrong side with an additional small square of fusible Interfacing to keep the prongs from poking through. Iron to secure.

ASSEMBLING THE BAG

1. With the right sides together, pin the Lining and Exterior Panels together, with the Exterior on top. Using a 5/8" seam allowance, sew around the perimeter of the Panels, leaving a 4" opening for turning along one long side.

> **IMPORTANT:** *When sewing along the area where the ric rac was basted into place, be sure to sew directly on top of the basting stitch. If you stray off this line, your ric rac will not be even and your basting stitches may show through.*

2. Trim the seam allowances to 1/8" to reduce the bulk, and clip the curved edges.

3. Turn the assembled clutch right side out through the opening from Step 1. Press so the edges are neat and flat.

4. Using the fold lines on the pattern as a guide, fold the assembled unit into thirds, ensuring that the snap lines up correctly. Press the folds flat.

5. Open the folds again and pin or clip the bottom folded section into place along each side. Be sure to tuck in the seam allowance at the opening so that it will be fully closed during stitching.

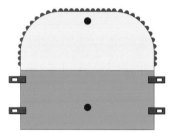

6. Beginning at the top of one folded edge just below the ric rac, edgestitch around the two short sides and bottom of the clutch, ending your stitches at the top of the opposite side just below the other starting point of the ric rac. Be sure to backstitch a few times at the beginning and end of your stitching since these will be major stress points on the purse.

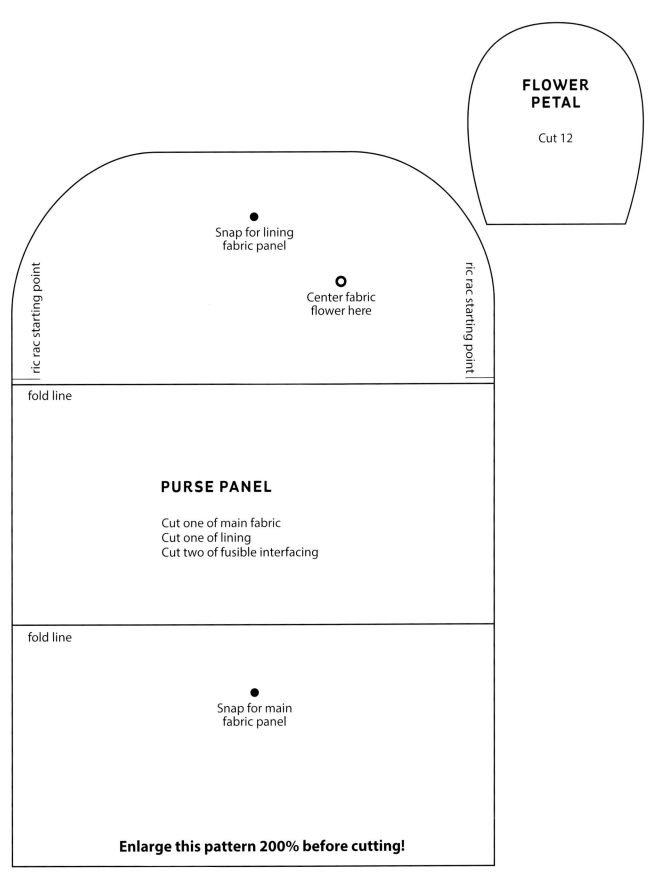

FLOWER PETAL

Cut 12

Snap for lining
fabric panel

Center fabric
flower here

ric rac starting point

ric rac starting point

fold line

PURSE PANEL

Cut one of main fabric
Cut one of lining
Cut two of fusible interfacing

fold line

Snap for main
fabric panel

Enlarge this pattern 200% before cutting!

BY SUSANNE WOODS

Finished Size: varies

MATERIALS

A variety of scraps of quilting cotton, approximately 6" square

Medium weight fusible Interfacing:
(2) 6" squares for each Fruit

Marking tool

Embroidery needle

For the Apple, Peach & Eggplant:
(1) 3" length of 1" wide brown single fold bias tape
(1) 4½" square of Green Felt
Green embroidery floss

For the Watermelon:
9 black snaps or seed beads
Black all-purpose thread

FRUITY GIFT CARD HOLDERS

We all buy gift cards from time to time. If you are like me and worry that they may not seem as thoughtful as they could, why not combine them with a little handmade? These fruits are sure to be appropriate for any occasion—an apple for the teacher, a peach for your peach-of-a-coach, a watermelon for a kid's birthday and even an eggplant for...well, maybe I'm not sure what occasion that would be for, but it sure is cute!

Zig zag stitching to just shy of the width of your card ensures a snug fit and the extra hand-stitched details on each, add thoughtfulness in every stitch.

PREPARATION

1. Photocopy (following the enlargement instructions) 2 copies of the appropriate Fruit pattern (see page 25). Cut out 1 Main and 1 Pocket pattern for each fruit.

2. For each shape, select 3 different fabrics: a Main, a Pocket and a Backing.

> **TIP:** *Want to really get scrappy? Follow what I did for my eggplant and create a pieced Main Fabric.*

3. Fuse the Interfacing to the wrong side of the Main and Backing fabrics.

4. Position the pattern, print side up, on the right side of the corresponding Main and Pocket fabrics. Pin into place and cut the shapes.

5. Flip over the Main pattern so that the type is face down on the right side of the Backing fabric and repeat Step 4.

6. Fold the top raw edge of the Pocket over by ¼" so that the wrong sides are together. Press and edgestitch along the fold.

> **TIP:** *When folding over a curved Pocket on the Peach or the Watermelon, mark your ¼" seam allowance on the wrong side of the Pocket fabric, clip the curves to just shy of the drawn line and add a thin strip of white glue to secure the curve into place before edgestitching.*

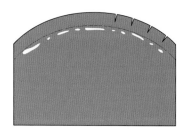

7. Position the assembled Pocket on top of the Main fabric, both right sides facing up. Baste the Pocket along the outer raw edges using a ⅛" seam allowance.

Follow the instructions for the corresponding fruit.

THE APPLE

1. Cut a 3" length of bias tape. Fold in half, short ends and wrong sides together. Press.

> **TIP:** *These are so quick to make, why not make a dozen! Join with the other parents in your children's class to collect a dozen gift cards from the teacher's favorite places and make a gift card wreath. Suspend them from the bias tape stems and you'll be the Teacher's Pet in no time!*

2. Position the Backing fabric and the assembled Main/Pocket unit right sides together. Stitch around the entire shape leaving a 3" opening along the top for turning. Clip around the curves.

3. Turn the Apple right side out and use a blunt object like a chopstick to gently push out the seams.

4. Tuck in the seam allowances from the opening and press. Insert the folded Stem from Step 1 into the top of the Apple shape in your desired position and pin in place.

5. Edgestitch around the entire top half of the shape being sure to enclose the seam allowance of the opening and attaching the Stem as you sew.

6. Adjust your machine to a zig zag stitch and sew along each side of the Pocket and the Main fabrics. Allow about ½" on both sides, securing the Pocket nicely and ensuring a snug fit for the card.

7. Photocopy and cut out the Leaf pattern (see page 139). Then, cut out a Leaf shape from the Green Felt. Transfer the vein markings from the pattern using a water soluble marker. Use the green embroidery floss and a simple running stitch (see page 7) to embroider the vein pattern and attach to your Apple with a few tacking stitches.

THE PEACH

1. Cut a 3" length of bias tape. Fold in half, long edges and wrong sides together. Press. Fold in half again, this time with the short ends together. Press.

2. Follow Steps 2-7 from the Apple, extending the zig zag stitch to approximately 1" on both sides of the Pocket.

THE EGGPLANT

1. Cut a 3" length of bias tape. Fold in half, long edges and wrong sides together. Press. Fold in half again, this time with the short ends together and press.

2. Follow Steps 2-6 from the Apple, extending the zig zag stitch to approximately 1" on both sides of the Pocket.

3. Photocopy and cut out the Eggplant Top pattern (see facing page). Cut out a Top shape from the Green Felt. Use the green embroidery floss and a simple running stitch (see page 7) to attach the Top to just the Main and Pocket fabrics being careful not to go through to the Backing fabric.

THE WATERMELON

1. Follow Steps 2 and 3 from the Apple, omitting the stem.

2. Tuck in the seam allowances from the opening, press and pin in place.

3. Edgestitch around the entire top half of the shape being sure to enclose the seam allowance of the opening as you sew.

4. Change to a zig zag stitch and sew along each side of the Pocket and the Main fabrics about 1" on both sides. This secures the Pocket nicely and ensures a snug fit for the card.

5. Using a black all-purpose thread (or hot glue if preferred), sew the snaps or seed beads to just the Pocket fabric in a pleasing arrangement. If hand stitching on, be careful not to go through to the Main fabric as this will stitch the Pocket closed. There should be enough room inside the Pocket for the needle to do this and I like waiting until the holder is assembled before deciding on the final placement of the 'seeds.'

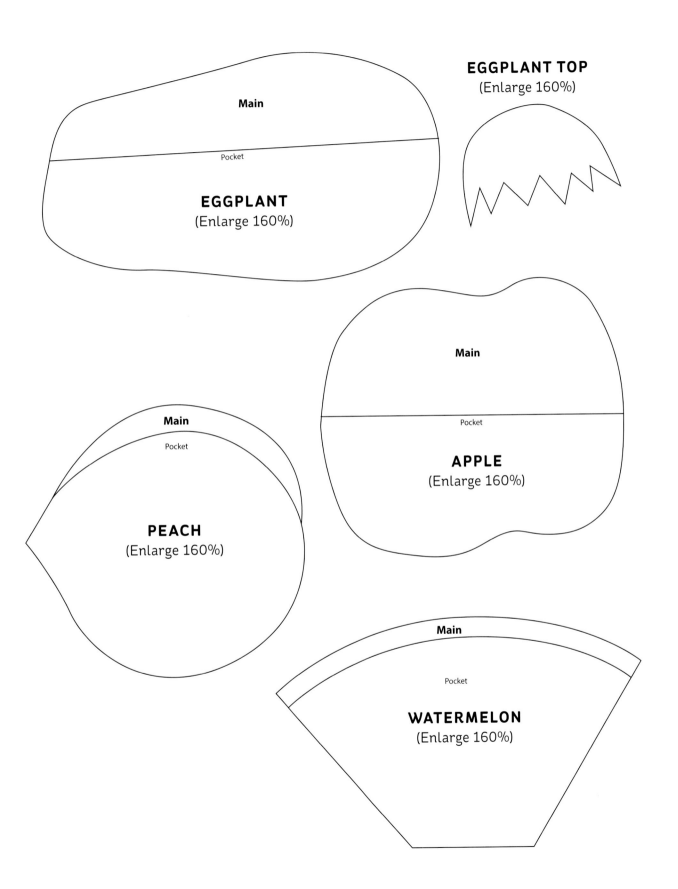

Main

Pocket

EGGPLANT
(Enlarge 160%)

EGGPLANT TOP
(Enlarge 160%)

Main

Pocket

APPLE
(Enlarge 160%)

Main

Pocket

PEACH
(Enlarge 160%)

Main

Pocket

WATERMELON
(Enlarge 160%)

DRAWSTRING BAG

Whenever I travel, I feel like I have charger cords everywhere. This sweet drawstring bag is about containing the crazy and getting to travel with some cute fabric. I've discovered that these bags are also the perfect size to hold all sorts of things, from kids toys to hand stitching projects. Plastic bags will be a thing of the past. They also make great gift bags! If you have a young sewist in your life, this is a perfect beginner project to sew with them. You can also extend the length and add boxed corners (see page 11) if you like. It's easy to adjust the bags to whatever size you need; the Lining is always 4" longer than the Exterior. I sometimes adjust the size to the scraps I have on hand!

BY LEE CHAPPELL MONROE

. . . .

Finished Size: 7½" x 8½"

MATERIALS

Exterior: 1 Fat Eighth

Lining: 1 Fat Eighth

(1) 44" length of ¼"-½" wide ribbon

40 wt Aurifil (This weight works great for constructing bags.)

Water soluble marker

Fray Check

CUTTING

From the Exterior Fabric, cut:
(1) 8½" x 16" rectangle

NOTE: *If your fabric is directional, it is important to note that the bag will be folded in half along the 16" side so your pattern may be upside down on one side of the Exterior. If this is the case, piece together (2) 8½" x 8¼" rectangles with the pattern a mirror image to make the 8½" x 16" Exterior.*

From the Lining Fabric, cut:
(1) 8½" x 20" rectangle

From the ribbon, cut:
(2) 22" lengths

ASSEMBLING THE EXTERIOR

1. Position the Exterior and Lining rectangles right sides together aligning an 8½" edge and stitch. Repeat for the second 8½" edge forming a tube. Note that the Lining is 4" longer, so the rectangles will not align lengthwise.

2. With the wrong sides of the fabrics still facing together, align the two seams from Step 1. Press the seams towards the Exterior. Pin the seams in place.

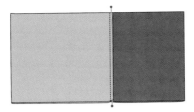

3. On the wrong side along the raw edge of the Lining, measure 2" away from the pinned seams. Mark using a water soluble marker.

4. Beginning at the drawn line and using a ½" seam allowance, sew along the raw edge of the Lining, being sure to backstitch at the beginning and knot at the end. Repeat for the opposite side.

5. Repeat Step 4 along the raw edges of the Exterior, beginning at the pinned seam instead of the drawn line from Step 3.

6. Turn the piece right side out through one of the 2" openings in the Lining.

FINISHING THE BAG

1. Press the Exterior as well as the seam allowance at the 2" openings in the Lining. Don't press the remaining Lining.

2. Stuff the Lining neatly into the Exterior with 1" of the folded Lining remaining exposed. This will be the drawstring casing. Pin the sides so that the openings of the Linings align. Ensure that the seam allowance of the casing opening is neatly tucked inside and laying flat. Press.

3. Topstitch through the Exterior and the Lining along the edge of the Exterior all the way around the top of the bag.

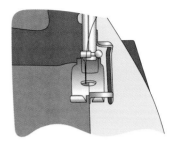

4. Pull the threads to the Lining and knot.

5. Attach a safety pin to one end of one length of ribbon and feed it through both of the Lining casings, coming out at the same opening. This creates a 'U'. Make sure there are no twists in your ribbon.

6. Beginning at the opposite casing opening, thread the second length of ribbon through both Lining casings, so that the ends meet on the opposite side of the bag as in Step 5. Make sure the ribbons do not cross one another.

7. Knot each short end of the ribbon lengths and add Fray Check to each raw edge to prevent unraveling.

EVERYDAY WALLET

Everyone needs a place to stash some cash! You'll love making this basic wallet for anyone you know. It's easy to customize with embellishments like grommets or rivets to give it a more masculine look, or buttons and embroidery stitching for a more delicate feminine detail. Personalize with some initials using felt and appliqué (see page 7). Suiting fabrics work great for this wallet and are easy to upcycle from an existing garment as well. It's a great introduction to sewing with children, since there are a minimal number of pieces to cut and it is straight-line sewing. I think it's a great project for children learning about money and money management skills. A wallet is such a great tool for them to use and be responsible for. Consider gifting it with Svetlana's Mini Coin Pouch too (see page 122). Tuck in some cash and you're all set!

8

BY ANNA GRAHAM

....

Finished Size: 3½" x 4½"

MATERIALS

Exterior: ¼ yard (fall suiting fabric, tweed, plaids, etc., quilting cotton, canvas)

Lining: 1 Fat Quarter

Scrap of leather (optional)

Rivets and/or grommet (optional)

8½" x 4" scrap of fusible woven Interfacing

Water soluble marker

CUTTING

From the Exterior Fabric, cut:
(1) 8½" wide by 4" tall rectangle

From the Lining Fabric, cut:
(1) 8½" x 4" rectangle for the Main Lining
(1) 8½" x 3¾" rectangle for the Card Lining
(1) 8½" x 9¾" rectangle for the Card Slot

ASSEMBLING THE WALLET

1. Position the Card Slot rectangle right side up and, using a water soluble marker, measure and mark horizontal lines 2¼", 3¾", 5¾", and 7¼" from the top 8½" edge.

2. Fold the rectangle like an accordion using the marked lines as a guide. The finished piece will measure 3¾" tall by 8½" wide. Press.

3. Finger press in half, aligning the 3¾" sides to find the vertical center.

4. Sew two rows of stitching down either side of the center of the Card Slot with the rows spaced about ¾" apart. You should now have four card slots.

5. Align the top edges of the assembled Card Slot with the top edge of the Card Lining rectangle, right sides together. Sew along the top edge.

6. Position the fabrics wrong sides together and press.

7. Edgestitch along the top edge.

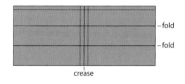

8. With both right sides up, position the assembled unit from Step 7 on top of the Main Lining, aligning the bottom raw edges. Set aside.

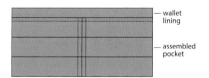

9. Fuse the Interfacing to the wrong side of the Exterior rectangle.

10. Position the unit from Step 8 and Exterior rectangle, right sides together, and sew around all sides leaving a 3" opening for turning. Clip the corners. Press.

11. Turn the wallet right side out and edgestitch around the entire wallet.

> **TIP:** *I use a chopstick to guide the wallet through the feed dogs. This allows you to get really close around the corners since it helps grab onto the feed dogs of your sewing machine. You'll be sewing close to the top of the pocket, but be sure not to catch the pocket (with wallet slots) when topstitching.*

12. Press well and add optional embellishment, grommets, leather, rivets or buttons following the manufacturer's instructions for the hardware.

> **TIP:** *For one of my wallets, I used a 2" square of leather and a 1" grommet to embellish the front. If you choose to do the same, be sure to only punch a hole for the grommet through the Exterior and Lining fabrics, not the Card Slot. Get creative and attach buttons, beads, or even patches to personalize the wallet for your lucky recipient.*

BY LINDSEY NEILL AND AROMRAK LUANGRATH

....

Finished Size: 7"

MATERIALS

Donut: ⅜ yard

Frosting: 6½" square

Center Circle: 3" square

(1) 10" square for the Backing

(1) 10" square of Insul-Brite

¼" yard of 20" wide HeatnBond Lite Interfacing

Water soluble marker

¾" (#18) Bias tape maker (optional)

CUTTING

From the Donut Fabric, cut:
(1) 8" square
(1) 13" square for bias binding, then subcut and assemble:
45" of 1½" strips cut on the bias

From the HeatnBond Lite, cut:
(1) 6½" square
(1) 3" square

PREPARING THE BIAS TAPE

Sew the 1½" bias strips together. Fold and press using a bias tape maker, or fold the long edges together to create a center crease. Then, open the fold and bring both long edges to the center crease and press to create 1¼ yard of ¾" double fold bias tape (1½" wide unfolded).

ASSEMBLING THE POTHOLDER

1. Fuse the 6½" square of Interfacing to the wrong side of the Frosting square and the 3" square of Interfacing to the wrong side of the Center Circle square.

DONUT POTHOLDER

Our shared love of sewing and food has bonded our friendship for the past several years. Our first (but definitely not our last) sewing collaboration is this donut potholder. The pattern was born from the idea that combining what could be just a boring practical object (a potholder), with the classic shape of an internationally-loved dessert, could be the magical recipe for one yummy lite gift! This is a fun, quick and easy make, perfect for a housewarming gift, a college-bound high-school grad or a hostess gift.

Hit the novelty fabric aisle and have fun searching for just the right donut and frosting prints!

2. Photocopy and cut out the Frosting, Donut and Center Circle patterns (see pages 132-133). Using a water soluble marker, trace the templates onto the right side of the Frosting, Donut and Center Circle Fabrics and cut out all of the shapes.

3. Peel away the paper from the Interfacing, align the Center Circle on the Donut and fuse. Repeat with the Frosting fabric. The top of the donut should now be layered with the Donut on the bottom, Center Circle in the middle and Frosting on the top.

4. Using a blanket or zig zag stitch on your machine, appliqué along the inner circle and outside edge of the Frosting (we used a zig zag stitch and set the length to 1 and width to 3 on our machines).

> **TIP:** If your Frosting needs more color, consider embroidering 'sprinkles', using a Perle cotton. Make sure to add any decorative stitches BEFORE quilting all the layers together.

5. Position the Backing fabric with the wrong side facing up. Layer the Insul-Brite, then the appliquéd Donut top both with their right sides facing up. Quilt as desired (we chose a classic 1" cross-hatch). Trim off the excess Insul-Brite and Backing fabric.

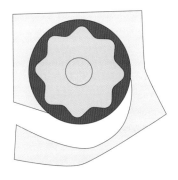

MAKING THE LOOP

Trim a 5½" length off one end of the bias tape. The loop should measure ⅜" x 5½". Edgestitch along the open, unfolded edge of the loop. Fold the loop in half so the raw edges meet, and pin in your desired location along a raw edge of the Backing fabric.

BINDING THE POTHOLDER

1. Open the bias tape strip and press one short end in to the wrong side to create a 90-degree angle. Pin to the right side of the Backing fabric.

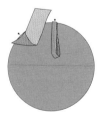

2. Continue attaching the bias tape around the circumference of the Potholder, following the curve and pinning as you go.

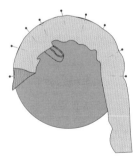

3. Align the needle and sew along the first crease (³⁄₈") all around the circumference of the Potholder.

4. Overlap where you started binding by ½" going over the folded 90-degree angled fabric.

5. Fold the bias tape over toward the Donut fabric, enclosing the raw edge.

6. Refold the bias tape so its raw edge is enclosed. Sew in place along the inner fold of the tape, backstitching at the beginning and the end.

BY JENNIFER MATHIS

Finished Size: 6" x 5" x 4"

MATERIALS

Exterior: 1 Fat Quarter

Lining: 1 Fat Quarter

¼ yard of Fusible Fleece

¼ yard of lightweight fusible Interfacing

Perle cotton

Embroidery needle

TIP: *Choose a larger scale print for the basket and a smaller non-directional print for the lining. A smaller print allows more of the pattern to show when folded over and a non-directional print means it won't be upside down.*

CUTTING

From the Main Fabric and Fusible Fleece, cut:
(2) 9" W x 8" H rectangles

From the Lining Fabric and the Interfacing, cut:
(2) 9" W x 9½" H rectangles

NOTE: *The instructions given here are for creating one basket.*

HOLD EVERYTHING FABRIC BASKET

This quick and easy fabric basket makes a great gift! Fill it with treats such as lotions and soaps for your mom, pens, pencils and washi tape for your child's teacher or chocolates and sweets for your best friend. Raid your stash for fun fabrics and prints and get creative with your fabric pairings. They come together in a flash!

ASSEMBLING THE BASKET

1. Fuse the Fleece to the wrong side of the Exterior rectangles and the Interfacing to the wrong side of the Lining rectangles.

2. Along a 9" length, cut a 2" square from the bottom corners of all 4 rectangles.

3. Box the corners using the Notched Corner Method (see page 11) on both the Exterior and Lining. Note that the Lining is longer than the Exterior.

4. Turn the assembled Exterior right side out. Place the assembled Lining inside the Exterior with the wrong sides together.

5. With the wrong sides together, fold the Lining down by ¾" so the raw edges of the Lining and the Exterior meet. Finger crease the fold.

6. Fold the Lining over the top of the Exterior once again, this time with the right sides together and enclosing the raw edges. Press. This creates the decorative accent band.

7. Using Perle cotton, stitch along the edge of the fold to secure the Lining to the Exterior. Be sure to catch the basket Exterior without piercing back through the Lining so the stitching won't show on the inside of your basket.

TINY BOX ZIPPY

Who doesn't love a good zipper pouch? The Tiny Box Zippy is the perfect handmade gift: useful, versatile and can be made in an afternoon. This Zippy finishes at 7½" x 4" x 3", just the right size to hold all your necessities, yet small enough to fit in your purse. The bias binding used to finish the inside seams also provides just enough stability for the bag to keep its shape, making it the perfect bag for a sewing or craft kit or to store your makeup in while traveling!

The body of the bag only uses two Fat Quarters, so this is a great project to showcase favorite prints. With the option of an accent pocket or back panel, as well as zipper and bias binding choices, you can customize this bag to be the perfect gift for any purpose.

11

BY MICHAEL ANN SHEERVE

. . . .

Finished Size: 7½" x 4" x 3"

MATERIALS

Exterior: 1 Fat Quarter

Lining: 1 Fat Quarter

(optional) 1 Fat Quarter for Accent panels if desired

2 yards of ½" wide double fold bias tape

1½ yards of 20" wide medium or heavy weight, fusible Interfacing

(1) 16" nylon zipper

TIP: *In this project it is important to use the right interfacing. I suggest using a layer of medium weight, such as Pellon SF101. It is easier to sew through but will result in a softer edged bag. A stronger weight, like Pellon CraftFuse 808, can take more time to sew but will leave your Zippy crisp and strong. Don't be afraid to use your favorite interfacing combination. Try something new!*

PREPARATION

Photocopy and cut the Top/Bottom Pattern (see page 143)

CUTTING

NOTE: *Please consider directional prints when cutting*

From the Exterior Fabric, cut:
(2) Top/Bottom using pattern
(1) 17" x 3" Wide Zipper rectangle
(1) 17" x 1½" Thin Zipper rectangle
(1) 4" x 6" Handle rectangle (optional)

From the Lining Fabric, cut:
(2) Top/Bottom using pattern
(1) Pocket using pattern
(1) 4" x 7" Back Panel
(1) 17" x 3" Wide Zipper rectangle
(1) 17" x 1½" Thin Zipper rectangle

From optional Accent Fabric, cut:
(If not using, cut the units listed from the Exterior Fabric instead)

(1) Pocket using pattern
(1) 4" x 7" Back Panel rectangle

From the Interfacing, cut:
(4) Top/Bottom using pattern
(1) Pocket using pattern
(2) 4" x 7" Back Panel rectangles
(2) 17" x 3" Wide Zipper rectangles
(2) 17" x 1½" Thin Zipper rectangles

Fuse the Interfacing to the wrong side of all of the Exterior, Lining and Accent Fabrics **except** *for the Lining Pocket unit.*

ASSEMBLING THE POCKET

1. Align the Exterior Pocket and Lining Pocket units along the straight edge, right sides together.

2. Sew along the straight edge, position the wrong sides together and press.

3. Edgestitch along the folded seam and set aside.

THE HANDLE (OPTIONAL)

1. Fold the short ends of the Handle over ¼" to the wrong side and press.

2. Press in half lengthwise. Open the Handle, then fold each long edge, wrong sides together, to meet at the center crease.

3. Refold along the center crease from Step 2 so all the raw edges are enclosed and then press. Edgestitch around the entire Handle.

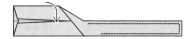

4. Fold the Exterior Fabric Top in half in each direction to find the center.

5. Center the Handle on the Exterior Top along the fold lines. Move each end of the Handle in about ½" to lift it off the Exterior Fabric Top a little so that the short ends of the Handle edge are about 2" away from the Exterior Fabric Top edge.

6. Pin and sew, creating a ½" x 1" rectangle with an 'X' in the middle.

PREPARING THE TOP AND BOTTOM

1. Position the Exterior Top and Lining Top wrong sides together. Layer the assembled Pocket onto the Lining Top piece, right side up. Baste the three layers together using a ⅜" seam allowance.

2. With the wrong sides together, baste the Lining Bottom and Exterior Bottom units together, using a ⅜" seam allowance.

ATTACHING THE ZIPPER

1. Omitting the Zipper Tabs and using the Signature Basic Bag Assembly instructions (see page 8), attach the zipper to the Exterior Wide Zipper and Lining pieces on one side of the zipper tape. Next, attach the Exterior Thin Zipper and Lining rectangles to the other.

2. Position your assembled Zipper Panel on a cutting mat and place a ruler on top of the short end, aligning the ½" mark with the zipper stop. Trim away any excess fabric, giving your Zipper Panel a clean, straight end. Repeat for the opposite side.

ASSEMBLING THE ZIPPER PANEL

1. Position the Zipper Panel on top of the Lining Back Panel, both right sides up and aligning the short edges at the zipper stop end. There is extra width included in the Zipper Panel to allow you to trim the long edges later. Therefore, the Zipper Panel extends beyond the raw edges of the Lining Piece by no more than ¼" on both sides.

2. Center the Exterior Back Panel with the wrong side up on top of the unit from Step 1 and align the short raw edges. Pin through all of the layers.

3. Sew along the short end, making sure to stitch right next to the zipper stop, not over it. Before pressing, reduce the bulk by grading the seam allowance.

4. To grade, trim each seam allowance smaller in succession.

5. Press the Back Panel away from the Zipper Panel and trim the excess width from the top and bottom of the Zipper Panel. There should be no more than ¼" to trim away from each edge.

6. Separate the Back Panel pieces, and position the Lining Back Panel, face up.

7. Position the opposite short end of the Zipper Panel right side facing up and aligning the raw edges. Pin the ends together. Since the edges were trimmed in Step 5, the raw edges should align perfectly.

8. Fold over the Exterior Back Panel, right sides together with the Zipper Panel on the short raw edge of the Lining Back and Zipper Panels. Pin the layers together.

9. Sew the layers together, again taking care to stitch alongside the zipper stop, but not over it.

10. Repeat Step 4, then turn the fully assembled Zipper Panel right side out and press.

11. Edgestich along the top and bottom edges of the Zipper Panel using a ⅜" seam allowance.

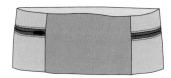

ASSEMBLING THE BAG

1. Fold the Zipper Panel in half, aligning the seams of the Back Panel. Pin to mark the two folds along the 3" wide edge of the zipper (not the 1½" edge) and at the center of the Back Panel.

2. Open and re-fold in half, this time aligning the pins from Step 1 and mark the other two folds.

3. Repeat Steps 1 and 2 with the Exterior Bag Bottom.

4. Turn the Zipper Panel inside out, aligning the four pins on both units. Pin the Bag Bottom and Zipper Panel together at the four points, with the right sides together.

5. Clip into the seam allowance of the Zipper Panel where it matches the curved edge of the Bag Bottom, spacing the clips between ¼" and ½" apart.

6. Gently ease the Zipper Panel and the Bag Bottom piece together, matching the basting stitches and pinning as you work around the perimeter.

7. With the Bag Bottom facing up, sew the two panels together, following the curve of the basting stitches along the corners. The ½" seam line should be ⅛" away from the basting stitches, so use the basting stitches or presser foot as a guide to ensure accurate alignment.

8. Trim the seam allowance to about ¼", and notch into the corners of the Bag Bottom to reduce bulk.

9. Turn right side out and finger press to get a clean finish.

10. Turn the assembled unit from Step 9 inside out, unzip the zipper and repeat Steps 3-9 to attach the Bag Top piece to the 1½" side of the Zipper Panel.

11. When pinning the Bag Top to the Zipper Panel make sure that the Pocket is facing the right direction (the raw edge of the Pocket should align with the raw edge of the Back Panel).

FINISHING

1. Cut (2) 30" lengths of ½" wide double fold bias tape.

2. Open the bias tape and, with the wrong sides together, fold over one short raw edge diagonally to create a 90-degree angle and press.

3. Position the outermost crease of the bias tape fold with the basting stitch line on the Bag Bottom piece. Carefully pin (or use binding clips) around the entire seam. Make sure that the fold stays within the seam allowance and is as close to the seam as you can get.

4. Stitch the bias tape in place, using the outermost crease as a guide for your stitching.

5. When you reach approximately 1½" from the starting point, stop and backstitch.

6. Trim the bias tape so that the two ends will overlap past the diagonal fold by approximately 2". This will create a smooth finish with minimal bulk. Repeat Step 2 on the other short raw edge and attach the remaining bias tape to the Bag Bottom.

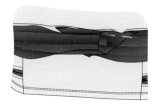

7. Fold the bias tape over the seam allowance enclosing all of the raw edges. Pin or clip the bias tape in place ensuring that the seam lines are also covered.

8. Finish attaching the bias tape by hand or by machine. Finishing by hand leaves a cleaner edge, while finishing by machine can be a bit quicker (see Binding Tips, below).

9. Repeat Steps 2-8 with the remaining bias tape strip along the other raw edge.

BINDING TIPS

BINDING BY HAND: *Using a threaded needle, stitch the folded bias tape to the Lining of the Bag Bottom. I recommend using a ladder stitch or blind stitch and try to keep your stitches as even and as discreet as possible. Stitch until you meet where you started. To finish, knot and bury your thread.*

BINDING BY MACHINE: *Make extra-sure that the bias tape is pulled a bit below the seam line when pinning. Then, with the already stitched side of the bias tape facing up, carefully stitch in the ditch right next to the folded bias tape edge. When you are finished, check to make sure that you caught all of the bias tape edge underneath in the seam.*

PATTERN WEIGHTS

It's always a joy to work with beautiful and practical tools. This quick and easy project is made from scraps of "too gorgeous to throw out" fabrics. I used leftover pieces of my hand-dyed shibori fabric, small pieces of scrap batting and 50 pennies – it's amazing how quickly these accumulate in a change bowl! Finally, I added a colorful accent and texture with some simple hand stitching in Perle cotton.

I love using small weights to hold patterns in place while cutting leather, vinyl or plastic, since pinning through these non-woven materials leaves tiny holes in the finished product. The weights are also handy when cutting stiff fabrics or a thick quilt sandwich, as in bag making, which would be distorted by pinning. They also prevent large paper patterns from shifting when tracing outlines.

These are perfect 'extras' for sewing swaps! Make a set of five or six in your recipient's favorite colors to assist them in their next project and they will think of you every time they use them.

12

BY DIANA VANDEYAR

Finished Size: 3" square

MATERIALS

Exterior Front: (1) 3½" square

Exterior Back: (1) 3½" square

Batting: (2) 3" squares

50 pennies or similar coins

Embroidery needle

Hand-sewing needle

Perle cotton #8, embroidery floss or other decorative thread

NOTE: *The instructions given here are for creating one weight.*

MAKING THE PENNIES POUCH

1. Sew the 2 squares of batting together. Leave a 1" opening on one side for inserting the pennies.

2. Fill the batting pouch with the 50 pennies.

> **TIP:** *I find that 50 pennies is the perfect number for providing a good weight for holding down a paper pattern. Don't worry if the stitches unravel a little at the opening. You will be securing them in the next step.*

3. To ensure that the pennies don't interfere with the presser foot while sewing, shake the pennies to the bottom of the batting pouch, away from the opening from Step 1. Sew the opening closed, overlapping the stitching with the previously sewn seam allowance.

MAKING THE EXTERIOR

1. Now is the time to personalize the Exterior Front. Use the embroidery supplies to add colorful accents and texture with some hand stitching. See page 7 for some simple stitches.

> **TIP:** *Stitch the designs as shown in the photograph opposite or create your own. For this project I used a Perle cotton #8, I love the texture it provides and it comes in a wonderful assortment of colors.*

2. With the rights sides together, pin the Exterior Front and Back fabric squares together.

3. Being sure to backstitch at both ends, begin sewing ¾" away from one corner. Sew along the raw edges using a ¼" seam allowance and leaving a 2" opening on one side for inserting the Pennies Pouch.

4. Trim the corners to reduce the bulk, being careful not to cut into the sewing line.

5. Turn right side out and gently push out the corners using a chopstick or similar blunt object.

FINISHING

1. Gently insert the Pennies Pouch into the outer shell. The weight of the pennies may break through the batting if handled too roughly.

2. Tuck in the ¼" seam allowance and pin the opening to hold the seams in place.

3. Using the hand-sewing needle and a coordinating thread, slipstitch the opening closed.

BY WENDY LUM

Finished Size: 3" square

MATERIALS

10 different Fabric Scraps (any type of fabric will work) approximately 7½" square or 4" x 8" strips allowing additional fabric if you are fussy cutting

Background: 1 Fat Quarter (I used a white woven)

Backing: 1 Fat Quarter (I used pink gingham)

CUTTING

From each of the Background and Backing Fabrics, cut:
(20) 3½" squares

From the Fabric Scraps, cut:
(2) 2" squares from each (20 squares total)

NOTE: *The instructions given here are for creating 20 Cards.*

MATCHING SCRAPS GAME

My girls love to play matching games, and they are really good at it these days. It definitely tests my own memory more than ever before! Over the years I had seen some beautiful fabric matching games for sale at craft markets and realized that this would be a great way to use up scrap fabrics. With this simple square design, cutting and sewing them is as easy as ... well, easier than winning a game of this!

For easy gift-giving, stitch up one of Lee's Drawstring Bags (see page 26) in a coordinating fabric so that those little cards don't get lost all over the house.

MAKING THE CARDS

1. Center a Fabric Scrap square onto a Background fabric square and pin into place. Using a small zig zag stitch on your machine, sew around each Fabric Scrap square, aligning the stitching with the edge. Lower the needle, lift the machine foot and pivot at each corner to ensure a single line of stitching and backstitch at each end.

2. Switching back to a straight stitch, position an assembled unit from Step 1 and a Backing fabric square, right sides together, and sew around the edges. Leave a 1" opening along one side for turning.

3. Trim each corner, being careful not to cut the stitching, then turn the card right side out through the opening from Step 2. Using a chopstick or similar blunt object, gently push out each corner from the inside to achieve crisp points. Press, being sure to fold in the seam allowance of the opening by ¼".

4. Edgestitch around the entire perimeter as close as possible to the edges. This will close the opening used for turning and provide a nice finished look to each card.

5. Repeat Steps 1-4 for all 20 cards. The quickest way to make this project is to complete each step for all 20 cards at the same time, assembly-line style.

CHRISTMAS PICKLE ORNAMENT

This pickle is a simple, hand-sewing project that will be a charming addition to your holiday décor. Why a Christmas pickle? Some say it's inspired by a German legend although that's debatable. To me, Christmas pickles are hilarious and I knew I needed to make one as soon as I first heard about them.

This pattern is quick and easy...and adorable. Just three pieces of felt and a whole lot of French knots. Not a fan of making French knots? Skip them and use seed beads or dots of fabric paint to add bumps to your pickle. Whatever you do, I think you'll enjoy making this to hang up or give this holiday season or even gift to the pickle-lover in your life 'just because'.

BY ABBY GLASSENBERG

. . . .

Finished Size: 5" x 8"

MATERIALS

(1) 6" x 9" square of Green Felt

Small scraps of White and Black Felt

(1) 48" length of Green embroidery floss or Perle cotton

(1) 12" length of Pink embroidery floss or Perle cotton

(1) 8" length of baker's twine

Fiberfill stuffing

Green and Black all-purpose thread

Hand-sewing needle and embroidery needle

Craft glue

Water soluble marker

PREPARING THE PICKLE

1. From the Green Felt cut 2 Pickle Sides and 1 Pickle Center using the patterns on page 131 and transferring over the markings using a water soluble marker. From the White Felt, cut 2 Eyes and from the Black Felt, cut 2 Pupils and set aside.

2. Thread the embroidery needle using 3 strands pulled from the Green embroidery floss or use Green Perle cotton. Make French knots (see page 7) spaced about ½" apart all over the 2 Pickle Sides and the Pickle Center.

3. Use a dab of craft glue to affix the Eyes to the Pickle Center. Thread a sewing needle with Black all-purpose thread. Position the Pupils slightly below center on the Eyes and stitch a '**+**' made of two perpendicular straight stitches through each one.

4. Thread the embroidery needle with 3 strands pulled from the Pink embroidery floss or Pink Perle cotton. Use five small chain stitches (see page 7) to create a smile centered just below and between the Eyes.

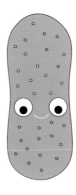

ASSEMBLING THE PICKLE

1. Position the 2 embellished Pickle Sides together, wrong sides together. Blanket stitch (see page 7) around the outer curve from points A to B using the inner line on the pattern as a guide for the straight line of stitching. Leave an opening as marked in Step 1 of Preparing the pickle.

2. Pin the Pickle Center between the 2 Sides, along the inner curve, matching up points A and B. Blanket stitch the Pickle Center to the Sides.

3. Stuff the pickle firmly through the opening, then blanket stitch the opening closed.

4. Thread the baker's twine through the eye of an embroidery needle and take a single stitch through the top of the pickle. Remove the needle and tie a knot for hanging.

> **TIP:** *Instead of French knots try using green seed beads or dots of green fabric paint to create texture on the pickle. Use additional felt to make a tiny Santa hat, superhero cape, eye patch, mustache or bow tie to personalize your pickle for the recipient!*

BY SHERRI NOEL

Finished Size: 4" x 6½" (closed)

MATERIALS

From both the Exterior and Lining:
(2) 4½" W x 7" H rectangles

TIP: *Label each panel: A1 Exterior Front, A2 Exterior Back, A3 Interior Front & A4 Interior Back*

(1) 7½" W x 7" H rectangle for the Pocket

(1) 9" W x 7½" H rectangle of Batting

(2) 7" W x 5½" H rectangles of Wool or Felt for the pages

Water soluble marker

Optional: Embroidery floss or Perle cotton #8 and hand-sewing needle for embellishing

Optional: Wool and freezer paper for the SEW appliqué

SEW NEEDLE BOOK

There's something so satisfying about being organized and having things right where you need them all in a pretty little package. Slow down and enjoy spoiling yourself and your friends with a sewing treat like this adorable needle book. It's one of my favorite things to gift to my sewing friends and the best thing is you can whip one up quickly using some felt and scraps from your stash. Sweet and adorable, this needle book is more than just a pretty package. The inside pocket holds needle packs and a pair of small embroidery scissors handy and ready togo when you need a quick stitch fix. Plus, the wool 'pages' keep needles at your fingertips while you're working. Add an extra personal touch by embellishing the cover with felt (see page 7 for transferring and appliqué instructions and page 134 for the SEW pattern). You will wonder what you did without it and your stitching friends will thank you!

ASSEMBLING THE COVER

1. With the right sides together, position (2) 4½" x 7" Exterior (A1/A2) rectangles together and sew along the 7" edge. Press the seam open.

2. Repeat Step 1 with the Lining rectangles (A3/A4).

3. Center the assembled unit from Step 1 on the 9" x 7½" Batting rectangle, wrong sides together. The Batting will extend slightly around the perimeter of the assembled unit. Baste the units together on the A1/A2 fabric edges using a ⅛" seam allowance.

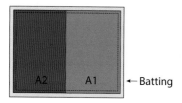
← Batting

4. Embellish the assembled Exterior as desired and trim away the excess batting. See page 134 for the SEW templates and page 7 for appliqué instructions.

5. Fold the Pocket rectangle in half with the wrong sides together to create a 3½" x 7½" Pocket and press.

6. Hand sew a running stitch (see page 7) approximately ¹⁄₁₆" away from the folded edge. Alternatively, you can use your sewing machine for this step.

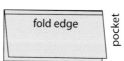
fold edge / pocket

7. Position the folded Pocket on the assembled Lining from Step 2, aligning the Pocket's raw edges with left edge of A3 (Lining).

8. Secure the Pocket in place by basting around three outside edges with a ⅛" seam.

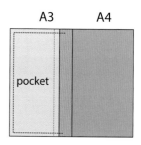
A3   A4
pocket

9. Using a water soluble marker, draw a horizontal line along the entire width of the Pocket, 2¼" away from the bottom edge. Using decorative thread and a running stitch, hand stitch along the drawn line through all the layers of the Pocket and Lining. Knot the threads at the back. Alternatively, you can use your sewing machine for this step.

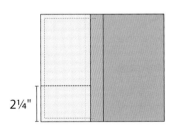

15

2¼"

10. Position the Exterior and Lining right sides together. Align the center seams with the A1/A3 rectangles facing. Sew around the perimeter, leaving a 2½" opening along the bottom edge.

11. Clip the corners, being careful not to cut through the stitching and turn the assembled unit right side out. Push out the corners using a chopstick or similar blunt object and press, being sure to tuck in the ¼" seam allowances of the opening from Step 10.

12. Whipstitch the opening closed or use Perle cotton to hand sew a running stitch along the outside edges of the back cover to close the opening and add a decorative element.

13. Being sure to center them on the right side of the Lining, layer (2) 7" x 5½" Wool or Felt rectangles for the book 'pages'.

14. Using Perle cotton, secure the book 'pages' by hand sewing a running stitch down the vertical center of the rectangles along the seam of the Exterior.

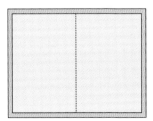

TIP: *When adding Perle cotton stitches, make one overhand knot at the end of the thread and feed the needle in through the top layer of fabric and batting, ½" away from the starting point. Pull the needle out at the starting point until the thread stops. Give a sharp tug until the knot pops through the fabric and embeds in the batting. When you finish the running stitches, and with the needle still on the Perle cotton, tie a knot near the last exit point. Feed the needle back into the exit hole through the batting and back out ½" away. Pull the Perle cotton through. Give a sharp tug again until the knot embeds in the batting, and trim the Perle cotton tail off.*

BY KATHY MACK

Finished Size: 7¼" tall, fits a 500 ml water bottle.

MATERIALS/CUTTING

From the Exterior Lower Band, cut:
(1) 10¾" W x 6" H rectangle

1 Circle using the circle pattern (see page 135)

From the Exterior Upper Band, cut:
(1) 10¾" W x 3" H rectangle

From the Lining Fabric, cut:
(1) 10¾" W x 8" H rectangle
1 Circle using the circle pattern

From Insul-Brite (or lightweight cotton Batting if preferred), cut:
(1) 9" W x 7" H rectangle
1 Circle using the circle pattern

From 1½ yards of 1" wide twill tape and the ribbon (if using), cut:
(1) 50" length for an adult strap or (1) 42" length for a child strap

Water soluble marker

Use a ½" seam allowance unless otherwise specified.

SEWING THE WATER BOTTLE CARRIER

1. With the right sides together, sew the Exterior Upper Band to the Exterior Lower Band. Press the seam open.

2. With the right sides together, pin the assembled Exterior Upper Band from Step 1 to the Lining rectangle along the 10¾" edge. Sew and press the seam allowances open.

WATER BOTTLE CARRIER

I was inspired to create the water bottle carrier after a family outing to the local 4th of July parade on Bainbridge Island. As we headed out the door, I found that my backpack was heavily loaded with everyone's water! These make it easy for kids (and adults) to each carry his or her own when you are out and about. Is someone in your family going on a big trip? These would make perfect gifts to send them on their way. Traveling abroad? Pair this with the Passport Wallet on page 70 and you have a coordinated Bon Voyage gift for the entire family.

The carriers are quick to construct and you'll have fun selecting just the right fabrics tailored to each person you are making one for. Looking to really travel light? Consider adding a simple pocket onto the carrier to hold a phone, hotel key, ID and cash and you are in for hands-free touring. What could be better?

3. Position the Insul-Brite on the wrong side of the Lining, aligning the top edge of the Insul-Brite with the seam from Step 2 and centering the sides of the Insul-Brite equidistant from the remaining edges.

4. Fold the Exterior fabric over the Insul-Brite, sandwiching it between the layers. Pin the layers together as you would a quilt. Edgestitch ¼" away along the sewn top edge. Quilt the assembled Exterior as desired. I quilted ¼" horizontal lines on the Upper Band and vertical lines on the Lower Band. Finish the raw 10¾" edge with a zig zag stitch.

5. Position a Lining Circle right side down on a work surface. Layer the circle of Insul-Brite, then the Exterior Circle right side up. Pin and stitch through all layers creating a pattern that looks like a pizza cut into eight sections. Finish the edges of the circle using a zig zag stitch. Set aside.

6. If using, attach the ribbon to the twill tape with a single stitching line down the center.

7. Fold the assembled unit from Step 4 in half, aligning the short edges and mark the center point on the Lining using a water soluble marker.

8. Measure and mark 2¼" away from both sides of the mark from Step 7. Fold 1" of a twill tape end toward the right side of the strap (ribbon side) and press. Repeat for the other end of the strap. Position each strap end with its folded edge facing the right side of the Lining and centering the Strap on the marked placement lines from Step 7. Sew the Straps into place using a square and an 'X' inside the square, enclosing the raw edges below the upper edge of the Lining.

9. Use a French seam to join the side edges. To do this, pin the short zig zagged edges together with the Lining sides facing. Stitch using a ¼" seam. Do not press the seam open. Turn the tube so the Lining fabric is facing out. Pin the side seam again with the Exterior sides together. Sew using a ⅜" seam allowance, neatly enclosing the first seam inside the second.

10. Leave the tube with the Lining facing out. Pin the assembled Circle from Step 5 to the bottom of the tube, right sides together. Clip or pin the edges of the tube ¼" deep to make fitting easier. This can be a little tricky, but just go slowly and add extra pins if necessary. Attach the Circle to the tube using a ⅜" seam allowance.

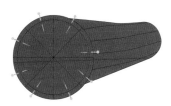

11. Turn the carrier right side out and you are ready to go!

BY SUSANNE WOODS

Finished Size: 4½"

MATERIALS

Exterior: 1 Fat Quarter

Lining: 1 Fat Quarter

(1) 5" length of 1" wide Ribbon or Twill Tape

(1) 5" zipper

Water soluble marker

CUTTING

NOTE: *Transfer all marks from the patterns using a water soluble marker*

Using the Belted Wallet Body pattern (see page 134), cut:
2 Exterior Body units
2 Lining Body units

Using the Belted Wallet Gusset pattern (see page 134), cut:
1 Exterior Gusset unit
1 Lining Gusset unit

ASSEMBLING THE BAG

1. Pin the Ribbon to the right side of an Exterior Body unit where indicated on the pattern.

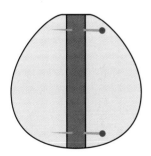

BELTED WALLET

The idea for this gusseted wallet came about during a family trip to Disneyland. Who wants to walk around with a big purse all day? All I wanted to bring with me was my ID, lipstick, credit card and hotel room key but I didn't want to just put everything in my pocket. So, I created this cutie with a belt loop so that I could position it on the front of my jeans for easy access (and so I didn't sit on it during the rides!). Have fun selecting the perfect fabric for an upcoming trip. If you pair this with Kathy's Water Bottle Carrier (see page 46), you have the perfect hands-free travel set for exploring museums, or a day at the amusement park.

2. Using the instructions from the Signature Basic Bag but omitting the zipper Tabs (see page 8), attach the zipper to the Exterior and Lining panels between the two transferred dots on the Body units. It can be a little tricky to attach the zipper on the curve, but use a few pins to keep the layers in place and stitch slowly.

3. With the zipper open, position the 2 Exterior Body units right sides together, aligning the raw edges. Using the two dots on the Gusset and the two dots on the Body for alignment, pin the Gusset into place on both Body panels along their curved edges. With the wrong side of the Gusset facing up and starting at one dot, stitch the Gusset to one side of the Body stopping at the dot on the Gusset. Repeat along the other side of the Body and Gusset.

4. Tucking the Exterior Gusset out of the way, repeat Step 3 with the Lining Body units and Gusset leaving a 3" gap along one seam on the bottom for turning.

5. Turn the assembled bag right side out through the opening, push out the edges gently and sew the opening closed. Press carefully.

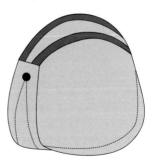

BY DEBORAH MOEBES

MATERIALS/CUTTING

From the Exterior Fabric, cut:
(1) 12" x 8" rectangle
(1) 6" x 8" rectangle for the Pocket
(4) 3" squares

From the Lining Fabric, cut:
(1) 12" x 8" rectangle
(1) 6" x 8" rectangle for the Pocket

From the ¼ yard of Batting, cut:
(1) 12" x 8" rectangle

From the ½ yard of lightweight fusible Interfacing, cut:
(2) 12" x 8" rectangles
(2) 6" x 8" rectangles
(4) 3" squares

(1) 10" length of ¼" wide elastic

Fuse the Interfacing onto the wrong side of every fabric cut.

E-READER COVER

This simple design takes very little fabric or time to sew, and is a thoughtful gift for any avid reader! Choose an Exterior Fabric with a good body like a linen/cotton blend. The reader fits right into the little corners, held securely when in use, or inside the interior pocket to be secured and buffeted when it's not. It works equally well for right- or left-handed users, and can be used as a dust cover for when you're charging, since you can still access the port when the cover is closed. This case keeps readers protected just as the dust jackets of yore, except all 21st century and stuff!

If you can ask without giving the gift away, be sure to get the exact dimensions of your recipient's reader to ensure a perfect fit. **This pattern is designed to fit an e-reader that is 6.7" x 4.6".**

ASSEMBLING THE READER

1. Cut the (4) 3" squares in half along the diagonal. Stitch 2 triangles together along the long edge. Turn right side out and press. Edgestitch along the long edge and clip off the little "ears" that are left over to make a clean edge. Repeat to create a total of 4 Corner units. The extra thickness added by the seam will add to the durability of the corners.

2. Position the 6" x 8" Exterior Pocket right side up. Place 2 Corners on the left 8" side. Aligning the raw edges, pin each in place. Layer the 6" x 8" Lining Pocket on top, with the right sides together, again aligning the 8" edge. Pin in place.

3. Using a ½" seam allowance, stitch along this 8" edge only. Position the wrong sides together. Press the seam nice and flat. The Corners will still have one of their raw edges exposed; no worries—we'll fix that later.

4. Position the 12" x 8" Lining rectangle right side up. Place the assembled unit from Step 3 on the Lining rectangle with both Lining fabrics together and aligning the three raw edges. The fold of the Pocket will be in the middle of the Lining rectangle.

5. Position the remaining 2 Corners onto the right of the assembled Pocket. Pin them in place through all of the layers.

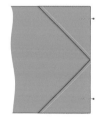

6. Position the Elastic across the right 8" side of all of the layers approximately 2" away from the raw edges. This way, it can wrap around either the front or back of the reader.

7. Layer the 8" x 12" Exterior rectangle with the wrong side facing up and finally position the Batting on top of the wrong side of the Exterior rectangle, making a tower of fabric. You've got a giant pile now, but don't worry, you're totally going to be great at it! Just attach some pins and sew slowly.

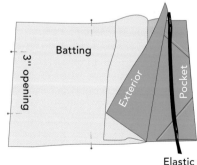

8. Using a ⅜" seam allowance, stitch around all four sides, leaving a 3" opening on the left side of the cover (the side that doesn't have all the corners and the pocket and junk) for turning later. Be sure to backstitch at both sides of the opening. Clip the corners to remove most of the bulk, being careful not to go through the stitches.

9. When turning the assembled unit right side out, be prepared to wrestle with it a bit. All that Interfacing and Batting can make for a lot of bulk. Push out the corners using a blunt object. If it is a struggle to get a clean point on the corners, turn

the assembled unit back inside out and trim a bit of the seam allowance away. It takes gentle pressure and some time, but you can do it!

> **TIP:** *I trimmed all of my seam allowances down to about ¼", with the exception of the side with the opening, which I left at ⅜" so I could be sure to catch the raw edges inside when I finish that edge.*

10. Press the cover like a crazy person. I mean, really steam it up. Keep working those corners with a blunt object, getting them as pointy as you can. Then steam them into flat submission!

11. Once the edges and corners are all tamed, topstitch along the entire length of the left edge (the one that makes the flap opposite the Pocket) enclosing the opening from Step 8.

> **TIP:** *Your seam should run from edge to edge, not just from the ends of the opening, to make a consistent final appearance.*

And there you have it! Padded and slightly stiffened, but still soft and easy on the hands. The elastic wraps around the front to hold the cover closed when you're not reading, or around the back to hold the cover open when you are.

BY VANESSA HEWELL

Finished Size:
4⅛" W x 5¾" H (closed)
8¼" W x 5¾" H (open)

MATERIALS

(3) ¼ yards or Fat Quarters: Fabrics A, B and C

(1) 9" length of ½" wide Elastic (braided)

¼ yard of Lightweight fusible Interfacing

¼ yard of Medium weight fusible Interfacing

¼ yard of Batting

Water soluble marker

(1) 3" x 5" memo pad

Optional: Walking foot

CUTTING

From Fabric A, cut:
(1) 8¾" W x 6¼" H for the Exterior Wallet

From Fabric B, cut:
(1) 7½" W x 5¼" H for the Memo Pocket
2 Curved Pocket units using the pattern (see page 55)

From Fabric C, cut:
(1) 8¾" W x 6¼" H for the Wallet Lining
(1) 7" W x 6¼" H for the Card Pocket

From Batting, cut:
(1) 8¾" x 6¼" rectangle

From Lightweight fusible Interfacing, cut:
(1) 3¼" x 5¾" for the Card Pocket
(1) 3½" x 4¾" for the Memo Pocket
1 Curved Pocket using the pattern (see page 55)

From Medium weight fusible Interfacing, cut:
(2) 8¼" x 5¾" for the Exterior Wallet and Lining

ORGANIZER WALLET

I'm a list maker at heart and created this organizer wallet with that in mind. It's small, but mighty with multiple pockets to help you stay organized. It's perfect for keeping up with a 'to do' list for your organized friends and relatives. Is someone beginning a new job? They can use this organizer to take notes and stash business cards at meetings. For the foodies in your life, this can organize shopping lists, coupons and store loyalty cards (for a really big gift, consider loading it up with grocery store gift cards). The exterior of the wallet is easily customized based on your fabric choices. It can be quilted using a favorite design, or it can be the perfect place to add some pretty embroidery (see page 7 for instructions).

This is a go-to gift you will be making again and again.

INTERFACING TIP: *Use a craft-weight fusible Interfacing (such as Pellon 808 Craft-Fuse) for the Outer Wallet and Lining pieces to give the wallet some stability. Choose a light to mid-weight Interfacing (such as Pellon SF 101 Shape-Flex) for the Pocket pieces to allow for some flexibility and ease in the finished Pockets.*

INTERFACING THE MAIN BODY

1. Center and fuse the Medium weight Interfacing on the wrong side of the Fabric A Exterior Wallet rectangle so that there is a ¼" border of fabric around the edges. This will help reduce the bulk in the seam allowance.

2. Repeat for the remaining Medium weight Interfacing rectangle and the Fabric C Wallet Lining rectangle.

ASSEMBLING THE CARD POCKET

1. Fold the Fabric C Card Pocket rectangle in half, long sides together and with the wrong sides together. Press to create a crease. Unfold the fabric and position the Lightweight Interfacing on the wrong side of the fabric to the right of the crease.

2. Fold the Pocket in half along the crease from Step 1 with wrong sides together. Edgestitch along the fold.

ASSEMBLING THE CURVED POCKET

1. Trim away a ¼" seam allowance around the Curved Pocket Interfacing. Center the Interfacing on a Fabric B Curved Pocket unit and fuse into place. This will face out in the finished wallet.

2. Position the second Fabric B Curved Pocket unit right sides together with the fused unit from Step 1. Stitch along the curved edge. Clip the curves and turn right side out. Edgestitch along the curved edge of the Pocket.

ASSEMBLING THE MEMO POCKET

1. Fold a long edge of the Fabric B Memo Pocket ¼" to the wrong side and press. This will become the finished top edge of the Pocket. Fold the Pocket in half with the short edges aligned and the wrong sides facing. Press to create a crease. Unfold the Pocket and position the Lightweight Interfacing on the wrong side of the fabric to the left of the crease. Be sure to slide the top edge underneath the folded edge slightly. Fuse into place.

2. Refold along the crease and edgestitch along the fold.

ATTACHING THE POCKETS

1. Fold the assembled Card Pocket in half with the short sides together. Press to form a crease. Open up the Pocket and using the water soluble marker, draw a line down the center crease. Position the Pocket right side up on the left side of the fused Wallet Lining, aligning the raw edges and with both right sides up. Pin or clip in place. Stitch along the drawn line and baste along the three raw edges using a ⅛" seam allowance.

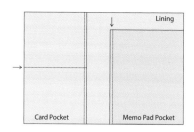

2. With both right sides up, position the Memo Pocket on the bottom right corner of the Wallet Lining, aligning the raw edges. Pin or clip in place. Edgestitch along the left fold of the Pocket through all of the layers, backstitching at the top. Finally, baste around the bottom and right edges of the Pocket using a ⅛" seam allowance.

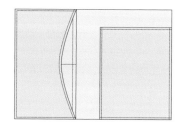

3. Position the Curved Pocket right side facing up over the Card Pocket with the raw edges aligned. Pin or clip in place and baste along the three raw edges using a ⅛" seam allowance.

ATTACHING THE ELASTIC CLOSURE

1. Position the Exterior Wallet right side up. If you are using a directional print, make sure the fabric isn't upside down. Measure in 1" from the left and make a mark at the top and bottom of the rectangle.

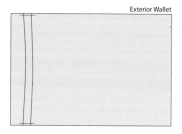

2. Position the Elastic to the right of the marks from Step 1 and baste it in place using a ⅛" seam allowance.

NOTE: The Elastic is slightly longer than the fabric. Be sure to align the raw edges with the top and bottom raw edges of the Exterior Wallet, producing a bit of slack.

FINISHING

1. Layer the Batting (bottom layer), then the Lining with the basted Pockets right side facing up (middle layer), and finally the Exterior Wallet with the Elastic attached right side facing down and the elastic at the right edge (top layer).

2. Using the Lining as a guide, trim away any excess fabric from the remaining layers as needed. Clip or pin the layers together ensuring that the elastic sits inside the wallet.

> **TIP:** *Using a walking foot to sew your wallet together can help keep the multiple layers from shifting and stretching.*

3. Stitch around all sides of the wallet leaving a 3½" opening along the side of the Memo Pocket. Before turning the wallet right side out, trim each corner carefully and trim the Batting to the seam line on all sides except the side with the opening. Trim the seam allowance to ⅛" on the edge with the Curved Pocket.

4. Turn the wallet right side out and press well. Using a slipstitch, sew the opening from Step 3 closed and press the wallet well to flatten and remove any creases. Topstitch along all four edges of the wallet, stopping to move the elastic band out of the way as you sew.

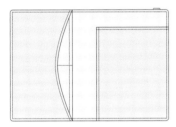

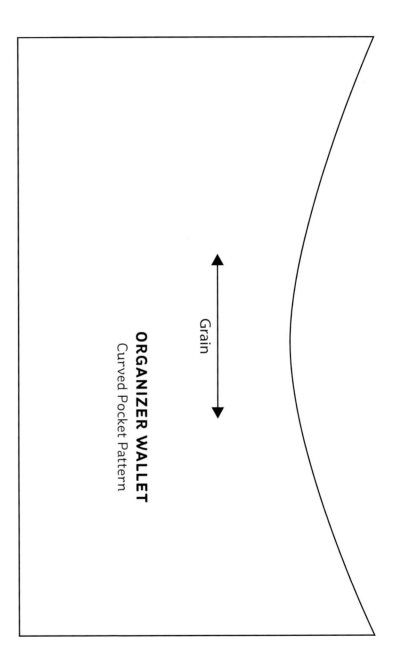

ORGANIZER WALLET
Curved Pocket Pattern

Grain

BY CHRISSY LUX

Finished Mini Size: 10" x 14"

MATERIALS

Ruffle: 1 Fat Quarter

Center Circle: 5" square

Background/Backing:
1 Fat Quarter

Binding: (1) 2½" x WOF strip

1 Yard of 1½" wide Twill Ribbon

Batting: 10" x 14"

Sheet of 20# paper

Sheet of cardstock

(1) 5" square of aluminum foil

Pencil

Washable white glue

(Optional): 2" round patch

CUTTING

From the Ruffle Fabric, cut:
(1) 3" x 21" strip
(2) 2½" x 7½" strips

From the Twill Ribbon, cut:
(8) 1½" lengths
(2) 7½" lengths

From the Background/Backing Fabric, cut:
(2) 10" x 14" rectangles

MERIT BADGE AWARD MINI QUILT

Sewing is awesome and so are you! This gift is designed to celebrate...everything! All those little (or big) victories that someone should just feel proud of. This mini quilt project is a fun way to celebrate anything from winning a band competition, to finishing up medical treatment, to landing that new job. Consider using a favorite pieced or appliqué alphabet to personalize the background quilt. I used a sewing-themed patch from Moda's Merit Badge collection as the center for my project, but this concept can easily be used to celebrate an achievement of any type. Crack open your embroidery supplies and hand sew a patch of your own to suit the award you are giving. This fun little mini is a welcome reminder to give the gift of affirmation any time of the year.

MAKING THE RUFFLE

1. Fold the 3" x 21" Ruffle strip in half lengthwise with the wrong sides together. Press. Using a ⅛" seam allowance, stitch along the raw edges using a long basting stitch leaving 2" thread tails at the beginning and end. Do not backstitch. Gently pull the top threads to create a ruffle.

> **TIP:** *If you have a good pleating foot attachment on your machine, you can also pleat your strip instead of gathering it manually, which can be a little easier depending on your machine.*

2. Copy the 3¾" Circle (see page 59) on a piece of 20# paper and cut on the drawn line. Use this as a guide to create the base of the award.

3. Arrange the Ruffled strip in a circle on top of the paper Circle and stitch together using a ¼" seam allowance leaving approximately a 1" diameter circle of paper in the center. Where the circle of Ruffles meets, turn the ends under and overlap them a bit before stitching. You can also hand stitch these ends closed if you like.

4. Carefully remove the paper, being careful not to pull out any of the stitches.

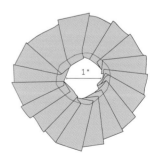

MAKING THE CENTER CIRCLE

1. Copy the Center Circle (see facing page) onto a piece of cardstock. Cut out the Circle.

2. Position the template onto the wrong side of the Center Circle square and cut out the Circle approximately ½" away from the cardstock edge.

3. Place the layer from Step 2, right side down, onto the 5" square of aluminum foil with the cardstock template centered on top. Fold the aluminum foil and fabric up over the edges of the template, little by little, smoothing out any wrinkles as you go. Using a hot iron, press the edges all around the Circle. Flip the Circle over to the other side and repeat. Wait for the foil to cool and then slowly peel it away from the fabric. Remove the cardstock template.

FINISHING THE AWARD

1. If using, position a Patch in the center of the Center Circle and hand sew in place.

2. Fold the 1½" twill ribbon lengths in half, short edges together, and press. Arrange the folded twill ribbons on the Ruffle unit, ensuring that the raw edges of the Ruffle are completely covered by the twill ribbons. Baste the raw edges in place on the Ruffle unit using a ⅛" seam allowance.

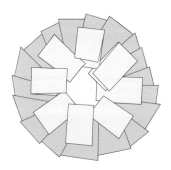

3. Use a thin line of washable glue on the wrong side of the circumference of the Center Circle. Position the Center Circle covering the hole in the Award, and centering it on the Ribbon unit. Gently press with a hot iron to secure.

MAKING THE TAILS

1. Fold a 2½" x 7½" strip in half long edges and right sides together. Draw a line at a 45-degree angle at one end and trim the fabric along the marked line. Sew along the raw edges using a ¼" seam allowance, pivoting at the angled cut and backstitching at both ends. Trim around the corners being sure not to cut through the stitching. Turn right side out, carefully push out the corners using a blunt object and press. Repeat to create the second tail.

2. Position a 2½" x 7½" strip of twill ribbon in the center, on the right side of an assembled Tail from Step 1, aligning the raw edges. Attach at the raw edge using a ⅛" seam allowance. Trim the ribbon to the desired length. Repeat for the second Tail.

3. Arrange the 2 Tails under the pleated Award and hand sew in place to the back of the Ruffle fabric, being careful to hide your stitches.

MAKING THE MINI

1. Position a 10" x 14" Background/Backing rectangle wrong side up. Layer with the Batting rectangle and then the second 10" x 14" Backing/Background rectangle, right side up. Baste using your favorite method and quilt as desired.

> **TIP:** *I quilted a 2" cross-hatch. Depending on your free-motion skills, consider personalizing the quilting by adding in the 'name' of the award or the award recipient.*

2. Position the assembled Award on the quilted unit from Step 1, being sure that the Tails do not extend beyond the perimeter of the mini.

3. Trim the quilted unit from Step 1 to the desired finished size (mine was 8" x 12") and set the award aside.

4. Fold the 2¼" x WOF strip of Binding fabric in half lengthwise with the wrong sides together, and bind as desired.

FINISHING

1. Position the assembled Award on the prepared mini, centering it with even spaces on both sides and at the top and bottom. Pin in place.

2. Carefully stitch through all of the layers around the glued Center Circle. Take care to keep the stitching about ¹⁄₁₆" away from the edge of the Center Circle. Do not sew the tails, as they should dangle on the mini.

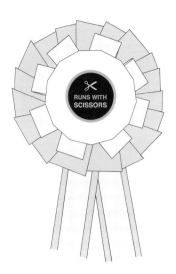

> **TIP:** *Take your time on the last step since you will have a lot of fabric sandwiched in your machine and will be stitching a fairly tight circle. Check your tension on a similarly sized stack of fabric to avoid skipped stitches.*

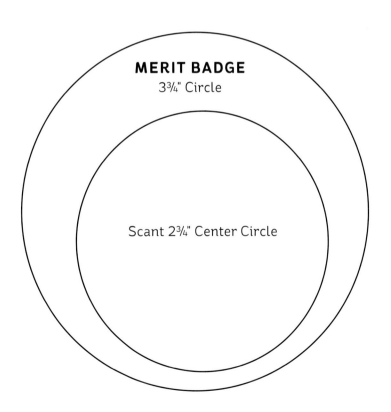

MERIT BADGE
3¾" Circle

Scant 2¾" Center Circle

BY AMANDA JEAN NYBERG

Finished Size: 6½" x 3¼"

MATERIALS

STYLE A

2 Fat Eighths Quilting Cotton

½ yard lightweight fusible Interfacing

STYLE B

1 Fat Eighth of Muslin for foundation piecing

1 Fat Eighth of Quilting Cotton

¼ yard lightweight fusible Interfacing

Several Selvages at least 13½" long

CHECKBOOK COVER TWO WAYS

What better way to celebrate opening that first bank account than gifting a custom checkbook cover?! Someone you know opening a new business? Replace their boring plastic cover with this cute and easy-to-make fabric checkbook cover. It only takes a few minutes to assemble and it is a fun way to use up some of your favorite stash fabrics. I made two different covers, but once you have the dimensions, the possibilities are endless. The first version is simple and straightforward, being made from just two coordinating fabrics. The second version, is made from fabric selvages. Feel free to use a lightweight canvas or home-Dec weight fabric in place of the quilting cotton for the exterior. If you use a heavier weight fabric, skip fusing the interfacing to that fabric only.

CONSTRUCTING STYLE A

CUTTING

From both the Quilting Cotton and Interfacing, cut:
(2) 7" x 13" rectangles

ASSEMBLY

1. Fuse the Interfacing to the wrong sides of both Quilting Cotton rectangles.

2. Position the fused fabrics right sides together and pin.

3. Sew around the perimeter, leaving a 4" opening for turning and backstitching at the beginning and the end of the seam.

4. Trim the corners near the stitching line, taking care not to cut through the line of stitching.

5. Turn the unit right side out, poke out the corners carefully using a blunt object and press well, ensuring that the seam allowances from the opening in Step 3 are tucked inside.

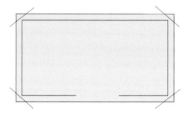

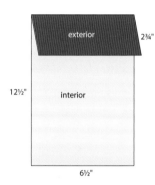

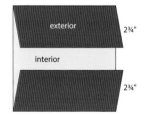

6. Edgestitch around the entire perimeter, closing the opening from Step 3 as you sew.

7. With the interior side up, fold over one short edge by 2¾" with the interior sides together and pin in place. Repeat for the opposite edge. Press.

8. Use a ⅛" seam allowance and sew along both short sides, forming two pockets. Backstitch at the beginning and the end of each of the seams. Trim the threads and your project is complete!

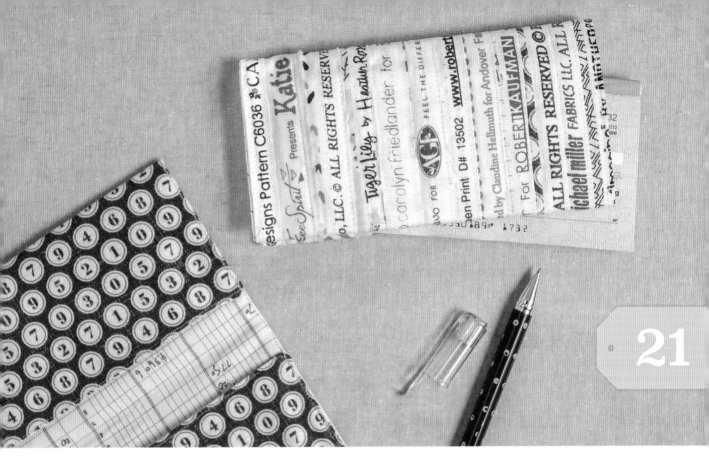

CONSTRUCTING STYLE B

CUTTING

From the Muslin, cut:
(1) 7¼" x 13¼" rectangle

From the Quilting Cotton, cut:
(1) 7" x 13" rectangle

From the Interfacing, cut:
(1) 7" x 13" rectangle

Cut or collect several Selvages that are 13½" long and of various widths.

> **TIP:** For a different look, attach your selvages at an angle using Nicole's instructions from her Undercover Maker Mat on page 125 for reference.

ASSEMBLY

1. Fuse an Interfacing rectangle to the wrong side of the Quilting Cotton rectangle.

2. Arrange the Selvages in a pleasing arrangement on the 7¼" x 13¼" Muslin rectangle.

3. Attach the Selvages onto the Muslin foundation, overlapping the edges and sewing them in place, one strip at a time. Press well.

4. Trim the assembled unit from Step 3 to 7" x 13".

5. Follow Steps 2-8 from Style A to finish the cover.

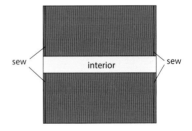

WATERCOLOR BABY BIB

When my kids were babies, it was such a bummer covering up their cute clothes with the cheesy bibs I could find at the store — so I made my own. I got so much joy out of making them for my children and it's even better making them with some fabric you've created yourself! Consider painting your own design using Dye-Na-Flow fabric dyes. These are perfect for decorating children's items because they soak into the fibers, and don't change the feel of the fabric as paints can.

Fabric painting not for you? What about using an orphan block from another quilting project, or that special piece of hand-dyed shibori from that class you took? Whether using a fabric you made yourself or selecting one of the many adorable novelty fabrics commercially available, a set of three or four is the perfect gift for a baby shower. And the thought you put into selecting just the right fabrics for your lucky recipient, will make your gift unique.

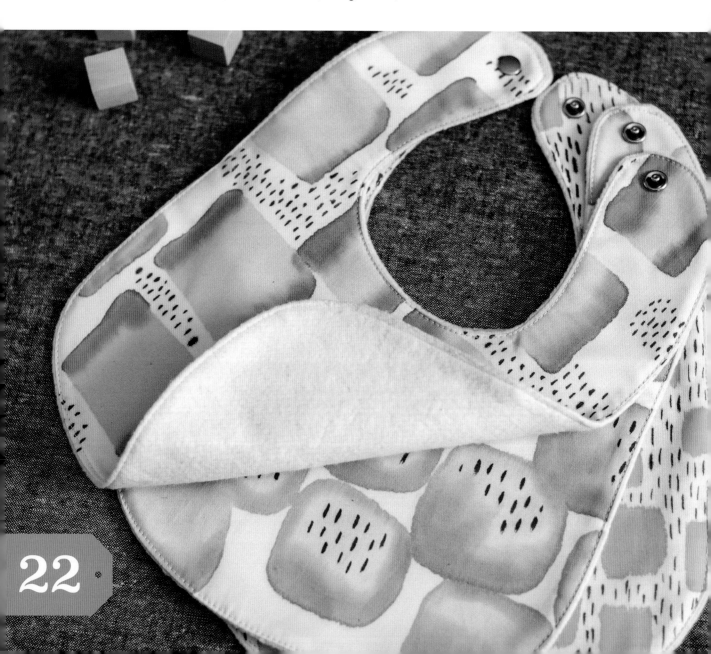

BY KRISTA FLECKENSTEIN

· ·

MATERIALS

Exterior: 1 Fat Quarter of white or off-white cotton

Backing: 1 Fat Quarter of cotton Fleece

(1) 1" length of ¾"-wide hook and loop tape or 1 size 16 metal or plastic snap

Water soluble marker

(optional) Dye-Na-Flow liquid dyes, brushes and cardboard

NOTE: *The instructions given here are for creating one bib.*

PAINTING THE FABRIC (OPTIONAL)

1. Wash, dry, and press your Exterior and Backing fabrics.

2. Position the Fat Quarter of cotton on top of a piece of cardboard and paint a fun design (see page 64).

3. Allow the fabric to dry completely, then heat set with an iron.

> **TIP:** *'Setting' is using heat, usually from an iron, to fix the color permanently to the fabric surface which ensures that the added element is both colorfast and washable. The amount of time for heat setting can vary depending on what paint or dye you are using. For Dye-Na-Flow inks, use the highest setting on your iron that is safe for your base fabric. Keep the hot iron moving over the surface of your fabric for three minutes to properly set the colors.*

ASSEMBLING THE BIB

1. Cut (1) 12" x 18" rectangle from both the Painted Fabric or the Exterior and the cotton Fleece.

2. Enlarge and trace the Baby Bib pattern (see page 65) onto the wrong side of the painted fabric with a water soluble marker and transferring over the hook and loop tape or snap placement marks.

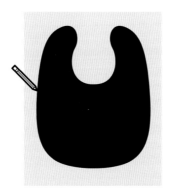

3. Position the Painted Fabric and the Backing together, right sides facing (the right side of the fleece is the fuzzy side), with the Painted Fabric on top.

4. Pin the layers together, aligning the raw edges.

5. Sew the layers together following the drawn line from Step 2, being sure to backstitch at the beginning and end of your stitching and leaving a 3" opening along one edge for turning.

6. Trim around the stitch lines, leaving a ¼" seam allowance. Clip and notch the curves.

7. Turn the bib right side out. Using a blunt object like a chopstick, carefully push out the fabric for a clean shape. Tuck the seam allowance of the opening from Step 5 to the inside. Press.

8. Edgestitch around the entire bib, in the process also closing the opening with your stitches.

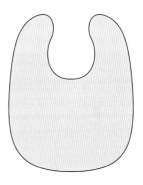

9. Where indicated by the transferred marks from Step 2, attach the hook and loop tape or the snap, being sure to follow the manufacturer's instructions that came with the snap set.

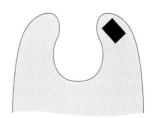

BERRY
1 tsp brilliant red
+ 8 drops black

POMEGRANATE
½ tsp magenta
+ ½ tsp yellow

MARIGOLD
1 tsp golden yellow +
10 drops brilliant red

MUSTARD
1 tsp golden yellow
+ 3 drops black

SMOKE
1 tsp white +
4 drops black +
6 drops azure blue

AQUA
½ tsp turquoise
+ ½ tsp white

LEAF GREEN
1 tsp sulfur green +
6 drops azure blue

MINT
1 tsp white +
4 drops black +
6 drops azure blue +
6 drops sulfur green

PEACOCK
½ tsp teal +
1 tsp white

PLUM
½ tsp midnight blue
+ ½ tsp magenta

BUBBLEGUM
1 tsp white +
6 drops hot fuchsia

CORAL
1 tsp salmon +
5 drops white

LITTLE TUTORIAL: FABRIC PAINTING

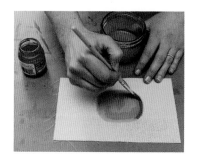

1. Gather some simple supplies: fabric paint, a small jar for mixing, brushes in varying sizes and a piece of cardboard to protect your surface.

2. If you are new to painting, begin with simple shapes. Using a combination of paint straight from the jar and diluted paint can result in a lot of depth.

3. Experiment with different widths of brushes to achieve the look you want. Above are some of my favorite mixes using Dye-Na-Flow fabric dyes.

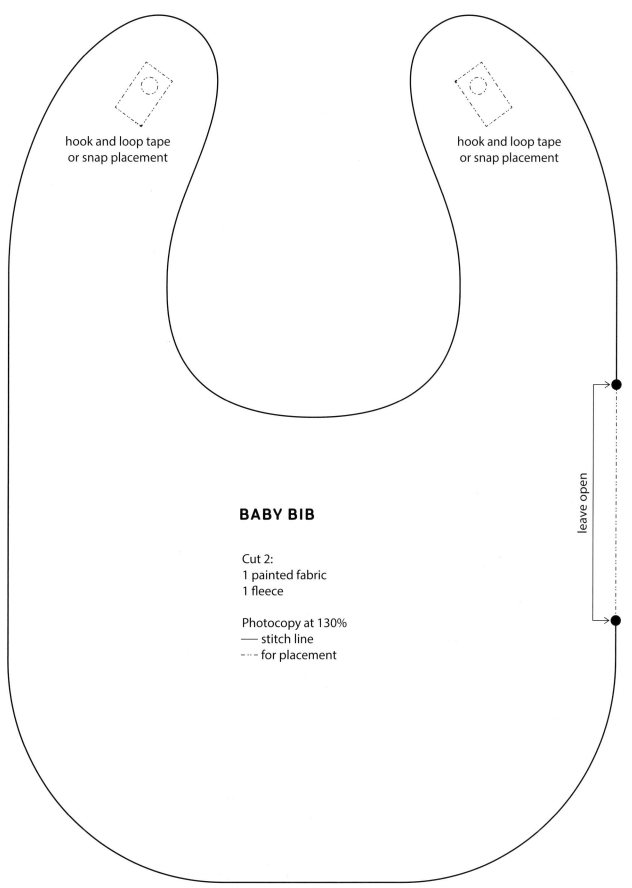

hook and loop tape
or snap placement

hook and loop tape
or snap placement

leave open

BABY BIB

Cut 2:
1 painted fabric
1 fleece

Photocopy at 130%
—— stitch line
---- for placement

BY SUSANNE WOODS

Finished Size: approximately 5"

MATERIALS

A variety of Scraps at least 6" square—7 for each coaster

(4) 6" squares of Felt

Sharp small-tipped scissors

20# paper

(optional) Water soluble marker

NOTE: *The instructions given here are for creating four coasters.*

ASSEMBLING

1. Using the Geode patterns (see pages 140-141) copy onto 20# paper and cut out. Use these as templates for cutting around each of the (4) 6" squares of Felt.

2. The layers of the Geodes are improv cut using the prior layer as a template. Using the cut Felt from Step 1 as a template, position on the first Scrap fabric layer. Pin in place and cut around the fabric.

> **TIP:** *If preferred, you can trace around the Felt onto the next round of fabric using a water soluble marker instead of cutting around the Felt itself.*

3. Using a sharp pair of small-tipped scissors, cut around the fabric shape from Step 2, removing approximately ¼" around the perimeter of the fabric and cutting more intricate formations if you like.

4. Position the cut fabric shape over the cut Felt from Step 1 and cut away a little more if necessary to see the layer behind.

GEODE COASTER SET

We all know that a set of coasters makes a fun housewarming, hostess, or swap gift and these are a trendy approach on that classic (and fun to make as well!). I created mine using an improv technique I'm sure you've never tried before either. I used four different colors for my set and also used a lot of metallic fabrics to try to mimic the crystals inside real geodes. Add some depth by alternating between the main color of the geode and a silver or grey solid, just like the real thing. For the coaster base, I used cuts from a felted, thrifted wool sweater and they add both the texture of the outside of a real geode as well as adding some friction to prevent them slipping around on shiny surfaces. Try using some metallic thread to really add that bling.

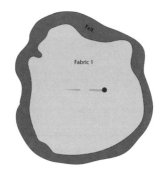 

5. Use the cut fabric shape from Step 4 as a template for cutting around the next fabric layer.

6. Pin the Scrap from Step 2 in place on the Felt and repeat Steps 3-5.

7. Continue adding layers by improv cutting and pinning until all 7 layers are completed.

> **TIP:** *Leave a good sized area on the top fabric stack to mimic the look of a real geode.*

8. Using a narrow zig zag stitch, and beginning in the center of the Geode, sew around every second or third layer attaching the raw edges and backstitching at both ends. This reduces the bulk of the coaster and leaves some of the raw edges which add the tiniest bit of crystal-like texture too.

> **TIP:** *I found that my layers stayed in place while sewing, but if you are concerned about possible shifting, feel free to fuse or glue each layer as you build up your geode.*

9. Repeat to create a total of four coasters.

24

Downtown Five & Dime
77 Main Street
19 40
DIAL 2-4387
Clerk
Account No.

BY HEIDI STAPLES

. . . .

Finished Size: 3" x 5½" (not including the Twill key loop)

MATERIALS

For the Small, Medium and Large Pockets, Exterior and Lining:
(1) 10" square for each

(1) 2" length of 1" wide Twill Tape

(1) 7" nylon zipper

Binding clips or pins

CUTTING

From the Small Pocket Fabric, cut:
(1) 3½" x 7½" rectangle

From the Medium Pocket Fabric, cut:
(1) 3½" x 8½" rectangle

From the Large Pocket Fabric, cut:
(1) 3½" x 9½" rectangle

From each of the Exterior and Lining Fabrics, cut:
(2) 3½" x 6" rectangles

ASSEMBLING THE POCKETS

1. Fold the Small Pocket rectangle in half, with the wrong sides and short edges together. Press. Edgestitch along the fold. Repeat for the Medium and Large Pocket rectangles.

2. Fold the Twill Tape in half with the short ends together, and stitch ⅛" from the raw edges.

3. Position an Exterior rectangle right side up and arrange the three Pockets from largest to smallest, aligning the side and bottom raw edges with each layer. Position the Twill Tape on the left side of the layered stack just above the tallest Pocket. Pin or clip around the three layered edges being sure to secure the Twill Tape at the same time.

KEY POUCH

There are times when all of us need to bring along just the basics without an extra bag and this little pouch makes it possible. A twill tape loop fits on the end of a key ring, and three slots allow you to bring along your ID plus two extra cards or a phone (adjust the width as necessary to perfectly fit your recipient's phone). The zipper pouch on the side is just large enough to slip in a lipstick and a bit of cash. I like to carefully fussy cut a feature print for the Small Pocket and then use coordinating basics for the other fabrics. Tuck a gift card into one of the slots to make an instant gift for teachers, college students, or your favorite person who's always on the go.

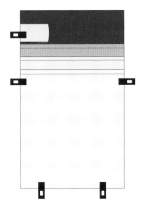 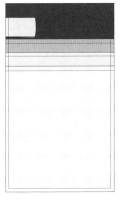

4. Using a ⅛" seam allowance, baste the entire stack together around the clipped edges, leaving the top raw edge of the Exterior rectangle unsewn.

> **TIP:** Try stitching along the side with the Twill Tape first, then the lower edge, and then the remaining long edge. Sewing in this order helps the pockets stay aligned and reduces the chance of shifting.

ASSEMBLING THE POUCH

Referencing the instructions on the Signature Basic Bag (see page 8), create the Key Pouch using the assembled Pocket unit, the zipper and the remaining Exterior and Lining rectangles. Do not box the corners or use the zipper Tabs and omit the edgestitching along either side of the zipper so that the Pockets remain accessible.

BY SUSANNE WOODS

Finished Size: 8" x 5" (closed)

MATERIALS/CUTTING

For the Exterior/Lining Fabric, cut:
(2) 8½" x 10½" rectangles

For the Exterior Pocket Fabric, cut:
(1) 7" x 10½" rectangle

For the Slotted Pocket Fabric, cut:
(1) 10½" x 17½" rectangle

From a ¼ yard of lightweight fusible Interfacing, cut:
(2) 8½" x 10½" rectangles

(1) 10" length of ¼" wide elastic

(1) ¼" grommet and installation tools

Water soluble marker

Fuse the Interfacing to the wrong side of the Exterior and Lining rectangles.

PASSPORT WALLET

Are you giving someone the gift of travel? I have just the project for you! I created this wallet when planning a family trip to London with a 10-day stopover in New York. When thinking about facing the scramble of the security line with two excited and probably tired young boys running amok, I knew we needed a single case to carry all four of our passports, my husband's and my state IDs for the NY leg, luggage claim tags and boarding passes all in one place. I used a fun travel-themed print for my pockets to add some whimsy to the case.

If you are looking for larger gift ideas for this one, consider an AirBNB, airline or a pre-purchased VISA gift card (perfect for travel, by the way—especially helpful to keep the kiddos on budget!) tucked into the bottom interior card slot.

ASSEMBLING THE EXTERIOR

1. Fold a 10½" edge of the Exterior Pocket rectangle by ½" with the wrong sides together and press. Edgestitch along the fold.

2. Position the Exterior Pocket from Step 1 on the Exterior rectangle, both with the right side facing up and aligning all of the raw edges.

3. Using a ⅛" seam allowance, baste around three sides of the Exterior Pocket.

4. Fold the assembled unit from Step 3 in half lengthwise and press to form a crease. Measure 3¾" from the bottom and ¾" away from the center crease line and make a mark using a water soluble marker.

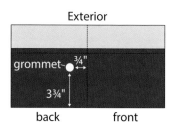

5. Follow the manufacturer's instructions and install the grommet at the mark from Step 4, being sure to go through both the Exterior Pocket fabric and the Exterior rectangle.

6. Thread the two raw edges of the elastic through the grommet to the wrong/fused side of the Exterior rectangle. Position ½" of the elastic on either side of

the grommet. Pin into place and check the elastic to make sure it isn't twisted.

7. Being careful to stitch only through the Exterior rectangle (not the Exterior Pocket), attach the elastic to the wrong/fused side of the Exterior rectangle.

ASSEMBLING THE SLOTTED POCKET

1. Fold a 10½" edge of the Slotted Pocket rectangle by ½" with the wrong sides together and press. Edgestitch along the fold.

2. Using a water soluble marker, draw a horizontal line 5", 8½", 11¾" and 13¼" away from the sewn edge from Step 1. Using the drawn lines as guides, fold and press accordion-style.

3. Edgestitch along the remaining two top folds and press. The assembled pocket should measure 5½" high by 10½" wide.

4. Position the assembled Slotted Pocket on the remaining Lining rectangle, with both right sides facing up and aligning the raw edges. Clip or pin in place.

5. Using a ⅛" seam allowance, baste around the three raw edges of the Slotted Pocket.

ASSEMBLING THE WALLET

1. Position the assembled Exterior and Lining rectangles right sides together, being sure the elastic is inside the layers.

2. Sew around the perimeter, leaving a 3" opening along the top edge for turning.

3. Clip the corners, being careful not to go through the stitching and then turn right side out.

4. Using a blunt object like a chopstick or similar, gently push out the corners.

5. Fold in the seam allowance from the opening in Step 2 and press the entire unit firmly.

6. Edgestitch around the perimeter, backstitching at both ends.

7. Fold the assembled unit in half along the long side and press to create a crease.

8. Open the wallet and stitch along the center crease from Step 7, backstitching at both ends and being careful to move the elastic loop out of the way of the stitching.

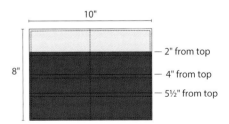

BY KRISTA FLECKENSTEIN

....

Finished Size: 16" square

MATERIALS

If dyeing your own fabric:
2 yards of PFD cotton muslin fabric
Synthrapol
Procion MX dyes (go to the jacquardproducts.com website to download dyeing instructions)

If using commercially printed fabric:
1 yard of Exterior Fabric
1 yard of Lining Fabric

NOTE: *The instructions given here are for creating four napkins.*

DYEING THE FABRIC

1. Prewash your fabric in synthrapol.

2. Cut the 2 yards of PFD cotton into (8) 18" x 21" rectangles. Following the manufacturer's instructions, dye each in a separate dye bath.

3. Wash, dry and press.

4. Trim each rectangle from Step 2 into a 17" square and decide which color to use as an Exterior and which to use as a Lining for each napkin.

USING COMMERCIALLY PRINTED FABRIC

Cut each of the Exterior and Lining fabrics into (4) 17" squares for a total of 8 squares.

DOUBLE TAKE DYED NAPKINS

In my house, we can never have enough napkins. Because of this, cloth napkins are the perfect projects for my dye experiments. A set of four napkins uses two yards of fabric. I like to use one color on one side, and one color on the other. This is a great way to experiment with different color mixes, dyeing times or chemical concentrations of your own.

If you don't want to mess with dyeing your fabric, simply grab a couple of ½ yards of four of your favorite fabrics suitable for the gifting occasion. These gifts are great for a housewarming or hostess gift, but also useful and practical for a birthday, office swap or Mother's Day treat. These simple napkins are perfect for adding a decorative trim. They would look adorable with some ric rac placed between the seams or even a pom pom fringe along one side too!

SEWING

1. Place an Exterior and Lining square right sides together.

2. Stitch around the perimeter of the square using a ½" seam allowance, leaving a 3" opening on one side for turning.

3. Press the seams to set the stitches and trim the corners.

4. Turn the napkin right side out and push out the seams and corners using a blunt object like a chopstick, or similar.

5. Tuck in the seam allowance around the opening from Step 2 and press gently.

6. Edgestitch around the perimeter of the napkin, closing up the opening in the process.

7. Repeat Steps 1–6 to create a total of four napkins.

> **TIP:** *Consider using a contrasting thread color to really add a custom look to your napkin set.*

BY LEE CHAPPELL MONROE

....

Finished Size: 7" x 10"

MATERIALS/CUTTING

From one Exterior, cut:
(2) 6" x 9" rectangles

From the second Exterior, cut:
(2) 8½" x 9" rectangles

From the Lining, cut:
(2) 14" x 8½" rectangles

From the Accent Fabric, cut:
(1) 2" x 14" rectangle
(2) 1" x 3" rectangles for Tabs

From ¼ yard of Fusible Fleece, cut:
(2) 14" x 8½" rectangles

(1) 14" nylon zipper

(1) 14" length of cording

Water soluble marker

ASSEMBLING THE EXTERIOR

1. Position a 6" x 9" and an 8½" x 9" Exterior rectangle right sides facing, aligning the 9" raw edges and sew. Press the seams open. Fuse an Interfacing rectangle to the wrong side of the assembled unit. If you are using the Fleece, you must press from the fabric side due to the thickness of the Fleece. Repeat Step 1 with the remaining Exterior rectangle.

2. From one fused Exterior Panel, cut a 3" strip off one 9" side and set aside. Leave the remaining Exterior Panel uncut.

THE DOTTY POUCH

Can you really ever have too many zipper pouches? No, you can't! Zipper pouches are one of the most requested sewing treasures from my non-stitching friends. Don't let them know how fast and fun they are to make! These delightful little pouches have a nifty cording accent with an easy to install method. Easily customize the fabrics and colors to suit your recipient or gifting occasion. You won't want to stop at just one; I often gift them in trios!

3. Fold the 2" x 14" Accent rectangle lengthwise around the cording with the wrong sides together. Sew a seam approximately ⅛" from the cording using your zipper foot attachment. The cording will be loosely contained in the Accent fabric. Trim the assembled piping width to ⅝".

4. Position the cording along the 9" edge of the 3" from Step 2. Using your zipper foot, sew just inside the previous seam on the piping, a little bit closer to the cording, but not quite snug.

5. Position the 6" Exterior Panel from Step 2 and the assembled unit from Step 4, right sides facing and aligning the long edge so that the piping is in the middle. Ensure that the color block seams of the Exterior Panel align. Pin in place.

6. Sew as close to the cording as you can with your zipper foot. Your seam should be just inside your previous seam and snug to the cording. Press your seam allowance toward the smaller rectangle.

7. On the sewn edge of the 3" wide rectangle, topstitch along the piping being sure to stitch through the seam allowance from Step 6 as you sew.

8. Position the Lining rectangles right sides facing, aligning the raw edges. Position the assembled Exterior Panels from Steps 1 and 7 right sides facing aligning the color block seams and one long edge. Layer over the Lining rectangles and trim all of the pieces to the height of the assembled unit from Step 7.

27

9. On a cutting mat, position the Exterior Panels with the smaller color block on the left and the edge closest to the cording furthest away, establishing a Top (furthest away) and Bottom (nearest edge). Using a water soluble marker, mark a point 1½" away from each Top corner along the top edge on the wrong side of the Exterior Panels.

10. Align a ruler with the mark from Step 9 and the bottom corner and cut. Repeat for the other short side and for both Lining rectangles.

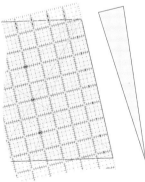

11. Follow the Signature Basic Bag assembly instructions on page 8, but before turning, box the corners using the Pinch & Cut method (see page 11).

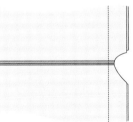

12. Cut away a small triangle near both sides where the zipper is attached to reduce the bulk after trimming the zipper tape. Be careful not to cut through the stitching. Be sure to stitch the opening in the Lining closed too. Push the Lining inside the Exterior and you're done!

PATCHWORK SCOTTIE DOG PILLOW

I saw my first Scottie Dog at the Elephant's Trunk flea market many years ago and fell in love! I've been collecting (and photographing when my bed got too full) vintage patchwork Scottie Dogs ever since. Just like old patchwork quilts, no two Scottie Dogs are alike—but they all have personality. I'm not sure where the pattern originated, but I figure it must have appeared in a popular women's magazine—possibly around the 40's—due to the proliferation of Scottie's out there.

Regardless, this classic soft toy will put a smile on anyone's face. Think of a birthday gift in your favorite little guy's team colors, a dorm-room reminder of home or a get-well gift for someone coming home from the hospital. This project is pretty irresistible and makes a refreshing change from that standard square throw pillow!

28

BY DENYSE SCHMIDT

Finished Size: 11" x 12"

MATERIALS

(54) 2¼" squares of a variety of Fabric Scraps

TIP: *I used a variety of colorful vintage wools and cottons, old and new, and tried not to repeat any fabric (except on the other side of the dog).*

For the Side Strip: ⅛ yard

Fiberfill stuffing

CUTTING

From the Side Strip fabric, cut:
(2) 2¼" x WOF strips

MAKING THE PATCHWORK EXTERIOR

1. Arrange the squares on a flat surface using the illustration below as a guide, ensuring that the shape of the Front and Back are mirror images of each other.

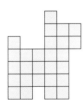

2. With the squares right sides together, sew the vertical rows. Press the seams up and down alternately by vertical row, i.e. up on first row, down on second, and so on. When all the rows are assembled, sew them together in order to make the Dog Front. Repeat for the Dog Back.

ATTACHING THE SIDE STRIP

TIP: *Before attaching the Side Strip, stay stitch for about 4" along the tail end of the Dog Back and about 2" along one side of each end of the side strip as a guide for hand sewing the opening closed later.*

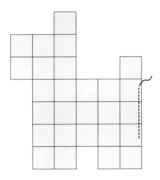

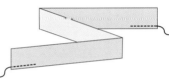

1. With the right sides together, sew the Side Strips together and trim to 55" long. Make sure that the seam is perpendicular to the sides.

2. With right sides together, pin the Side Strip to the Dog Front, beginning just below the tail end. If you stay stitched the edge of your Strip, pin the non-stay stitched side to the Dog Front. Sew the Side Strip to the Dog Front.

3. Make sure that the corners stay square by stopping and pivoting with the needle down, before beginning to stitch again. Clip the corner of the Side Strip. At the inside corners, stop at the seam, backstitch to secure, take the needle out and begin

sewing again at the seam line on the next square. Be careful not to catch the seam allowances with your needle when stitching inside corners.

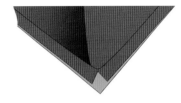

4. When you are near the beginning again, stop and sew the ends together, trimming any excess fabric, then stitch the remainder of the Side Strip to the Dog.

5. Repeat Steps 2-4 for the Side Strip and the Dog Back leaving that 4" gap for turning.

FINISHING

1. Turn the Dog right side out and stuff the Dog with the filling.

2. Turn under the seam allowance at the opening and hand stitch the opening closed.

TIP: *Consider embellishing your Dog. Button eyes are fun (remember you need two!) and so are scarves, necklaces or collars!*

Arf arf!

BY HEATHER KOJAN

Finished Size: 8" x 8" x 10"

MATERIALS

Exterior: ½ yard

Lining: ½ yard

1 yard medium weight fusible Interfacing

(1) 2 yard length of ³⁄₁₆" cording

(1) 1" decorative wooden bead

Water soluble marker

Piece of transparent tape

To make the drawstring work, you'll be threading 4 strands of the cording through the bead hole. The 4 strands of cording need to be snug in the hole, but still allow the bead to slide up and down the length of the cording. I suggest you purchase your bead first, then purchase the size cording which best fits through the bead's hole.

CUTTING

From both the Exterior and Lining Fabrics, cut:
(4) 8½" x 14" rectangles

From the Interfacing, cut:
(4) 8" x 13½" rectangles

FABRIC GIFT BAG

A few years ago, some kind ladies attempted to teach me to knit. They met once a week at a local coffee shop to knit caps for the newborns at local hospitals. I joined their group, and between sips of latte and nibbles of muffin, I learned to knit and purl. I was a quick learner, a slow knitter and absolutely smitten with my new craft. Soon enough, I needed all the things. And soon after that, I needed a place to put all the things.

So I created this bag. It's the perfect size to carry around a small knitting or hand-sewing project but it can also be used as a reusable holiday gift bag that becomes part of the gift itself! Fold in a Modified Infinity Scarf (see page 16) or a Tiny Box Zippy (see page 34) filled with art supplies. You can scale up or scale down this pattern to adjust the finished size of the bag (see page 81) to suit even the littlest of Little Gifts!

PREPARING THE PANELS

1. Fuse the Interfacing to the wrong side of the 4 Exterior rectangles, leaving a ¼" border of fabric exposed on the top and sides of the Exterior rectangles.

2. Fold an Exterior rectangle in half lengthwise and finger-press to form a crease. Using a water soluble marker and using the crease as a guide, mark the center point (A) on both short sides along the raw edges.

3. Referencing the illustration at right, measure 4¼" up from the bottom corners, and mark two (B) points. Draw two lines connecting point (A) with each (B) mark. Using a rotary cutter and an acrylic ruler, trim away the corner triangle along the drawn line. Repeat for the opposite side to form an arrow.

4. Repeat Steps 2-3 to create a total of 4 trimmed Exterior Panels. Set aside and repeat for the 4 Lining rectangles.

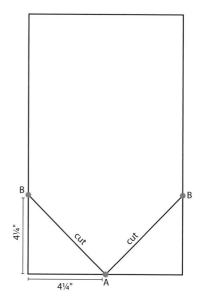

29

ASSEMBLING THE EXTERIOR

TIP: *Use a scant ¼" when sewing the Exterior and a generous ¼" when sewing the Lining of the bag. This will give your Lining a nice, snug fit.*

1. Position 2 Exterior Panels right sides together. Sew together along one trimmed angled side. Press the seam open or to one side. Repeat for the remaining 2 Exterior Panels.

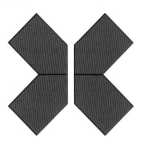

2. Position the assembled units from Step 1, right sides together aligning all of the raw edges and matching the center seam. Stitch along the remaining trimmed angled edges and press. Open up your assembled Exterior and it should look like a big 'X'.

3. Working with one side seam at a time, position 2 Exterior rectangles, right sides together and pin or clip in place along the long edge and sew. Repeat for all four side seams.

TIP: *Sew the first two sides together while the bag is flat then pinch the remaining sides together and sew.*

4. Press all of the seams well and turn the assembled unit from Step 3 right side out.

5. Position a piece of tape in the center of the cording to prevent unraveling and cut through the tape yielding (2) 1-yard pieces. Using a ⅛" seam allowance, attach one cording end to the right side of one Exterior Panel using the mark on the raw edge of the Panel as a guide for centering and aligning the raw edges. Sew back and forth over the cording 2-3 times to secure.

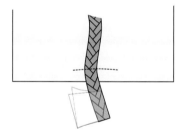

6. Repeat Step 5 with the other end of the cording and the Panel opposite the one from Step 5.

7. Repeat Steps 5-6 with the remaining length of cording and the 2 remaining Exterior Panels. Set the Exterior unit aside and leave the cording dangling from the bottom of the assembled Exterior.

8. Repeat Steps 1-4 for the Lining Panels, leaving a 3-4" opening along one side seam at Step 3 for turning.

ASSEMBLING THE BAG

1. Position the assembled Exterior and fit it inside the assembled Lining with the right sides together. Ensure all of the cording is tucked inside, in between the two layers.

2. Aligning the top raw edges, pin around the top of the bag, nesting the seams if you can and making sure that the cording remains perpendicular to the raw edge. Sew a generous ¼" seam around the entire raw edge, going back and forth a few times over where the cording is attached.

3. Trim all of the threads and any of the taped cording ends that extend above the top edge.

4. Turn the bag right side out through the opening.

5. Tucking in the seam allowances around the opening, hand or machine-stitch the opening in the Lining closed and gently push the Lining inside the bag Exterior, wrong sides together.

6. Bring out about ¼" of the Lining above the top edge of the assembled bag, leaving it exposed. Press the top edge and edgestitch on the exposed Lining close to the seam.

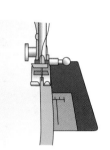

ADDING THE BEAD

> **TIP:** *The bead may be a little rough inside and might fray the cording. To prevent this, take a little piece of sandpaper, wrap it around a chopstick, and sand the bead hole.*

1. Fold one of the attached lengths of cording in the middle and feed the folded loop through the hole in the bead.

2. Take the second length of cording, and feed it through as well. It will be a little tight, but that is what you want.

> **TIP:** *A pair of tweezers will help to grasp the second loop. Slide the bead to the base of the lengths of cording, snug against the top of your bag.*

3. Align the folded cording ends and tie the tops together into a knot.

ADJUSTING THE SIZE

1. Determine the width you would like each Panel to be. Next, multiply the width by 1.6 and round up to the nearest ¼" to determine the height of the rectangle.

For example, if you wanted to make a much smaller bag with Panels 4" wide, then the corresponding height of your Exterior and Lining rectangles would be 6½". Cut 4 rectangles from both the Exterior and the Lining fabrics to your determined size.

2. Cut the Interfacing ½" smaller than the Exterior/Lining rectangle, so in our example 3½" x 6". Fuse the Interfacing to the 4 Exterior rectangles, leaving a ¼" border of fabric exposed on the top and sides of each.

3. To determine the cording length, multiply the length of the long side of the Exterior/Lining rectangle by 2.5.

4. Fold the rectangle in half along the short side to determine point (A) and mark a point on one short edge. For our example (A) is 2" away from each corner.

5. Using the illustration on page 78 and the same measurement calculated in Step 4 as a guide, mark two (B) points, in our example 2" away from each corner. Continue with the instructions for the project.

BY SUSANNE WOODS

Finished Size: 6" x 3"

MATERIALS

Orange Fabric: 10" square

Orange Felt: 9" x 2½" rectangle

Green Felt: 3" x 4" rectangle

White Felt Scrap: 2" square
(at least)

Lightweight fusible Interfacing:
(1) 10" square

(1) 18" length of ¼"-wide bias
tape white double-fold

Water soluble marker

White thread

Brown thread

Light green Perle cotton

Polyfill

Hand-sewing and embroidery
needles

CUTTING

From the Orange Felt, cut:
1 Peel pattern (see page 138)

From the Green Felt, cut:
1 Leaf pattern (see page 139)

From the White Felt, cut:
1 Circle pattern (see page 138)
and subcut in half

ORANGE SLICE PINCUSHION

Looking for a refreshing twist on a pincushion? How about this adorable orange slice? Using a combination of decorative stitching, bias tape and a textured wool (I used a thrifted sweater that I felted!), this pincushion is as sweet as they come. Oranges not your thing? Any citrus will work, or omit the white felt bias tape and stitching, add some well-placed black head pins and it can be a watermelon wedge! Use the green felt leaf to store hand-sewing needles, add some pins and it's ready for gifting.

Orange ya glad ya made one?!

ASSEMBLING THE ORANGE SLICE

1. Fuse the Interfacing to the wrong side of the 10" Orange fabric square.

2. Using the Slice pattern (see page 138), cut 2 Slices from the interfaced Orange fabric.

3. Using a water soluble marker and a ruler, transfer the segment lines to each Slice and the circle placement.

4. Using White thread in your machine, stitch over each drawn line from Step 3 three times.

5. Position one White felt half-circle on the orange slice as indicated on the Slice pattern. Using White thread in your machine, sew the half-circle to the Slice. Stitch as close to the edge of the felt as possible.

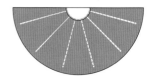

6. Repeat Steps 4-5 for the second Orange fabric Slice.

ASSEMBLING THE PINCUSHION

1. With the right sides together and beginning ¼" from the edge, stitch the 2 Slices together along the top edge aligning the White half-circles and being sure to backstitch. Stop stitching ¼" before you reach the end of the Slices and backstitch again. Press the seams open.

2. Beginning at the seam line and approximately ½" from the joined Slice seam, position the White bias tape ¼" inside the outer edge of the entire circumference of the joined Orange slices. Pin in place. Where the bias tape meets, fold one end under by ¼". Tuck the raw end under the folded end.

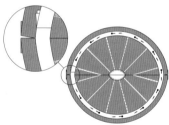

30

3. Edgestitch along both sides of the bias tape to secure in place.

| **TIP:** *It can be tricky to work with narrow bias tape. The Leaf will be placed over the area where the bias tape meets, so perfection is not required!*

4. With the right sides together, pin or clip one edge of the Orange felt Peel piece to one curved edge of the Slice.

5. Beginning at the seam line, stitch a ¼" seam to the opposite side, stopping at the seam line.

6. Repeat Steps 4–5, but leave a 3" opening in the middle for turning, being sure to backstitch at both ends.

7. Turn right side out, pushing out the tips of the Peel, and fill firmly with polyfill.

8. Hand stitch the 3" opening closed using a whipstitch.

ATTACHING THE LEAF

1. Referring to the stitch line on the Leaf pattern (see page 139), use the embroidery needle and green Perle cotton to backstitch (see page 7) the veins onto the Leaf.

2. Position the embroidered Leaf on the embellished slice, covering the place where the ends of the White bias tape meet. Attach the Leaf by hand, being sure to keep the stitches hidden and not to go through the front of the Green felt. Just a few tacking stitches will do.

BY KRISTIN LINK

Finished Size: Fits a pint-sized (16 oz.) wide or narrow-mouth Mason Jar.

MATERIALS

Insulated Fleece: ¼ yard

TIP: *I used Pellon Insul-Fleece, which has a layer of Mylar in between layers of polyester fiber, giving it both insulating and cushioning properties.*

Exterior Top: ⅛ yard

Exterior Bottom: ⅛ yard

Lining: ¼ yard

Fabric Scraps for the Drawstring Channels

cording: 1 yard, or you can make your own drawstrings with fabric or bias tape

CUTTING

From the Exterior Top, cut:
(2) 7¼" W x 4¾" H rectangles

From the Exterior Bottom, cut:
(2) 7¼" W x 4½" H rectangles

From the Fleece and Lining Fabric, cut:
(2) 7¼" W x 8½" H rectangles

From the Fabric Scraps, cut:
(2) 6" W x 2½" H rectangles for the Drawstring Channel

From the cording, cut:
(2) 18" lengths

ASSEMBLING THE EXTERIOR

1. Cut away a 1½" square from the two corners of the Exterior Bottom, Fleece and Lining rectangles and set aside.

2. Position an un-notched long edge of the Exterior Top and a long edge of the Exterior Bottom, right sides together. Using a ⅜" seam allowance, sew

MASON JAR COZY

Like many other parents, for the past few years I have been replacing most of my plastic food storage and serving containers with glass. Mainly, this means I am using lots and lots of Mason jars—for leftovers, cut fruit, soup and more!

Do you want to give the gift of baking? Fill one with the dry ingredients from your favorite cookie recipe. Looking for a gift for the coach? Fill it with her favorite candy and piece the exterior in your team colors! Go team!

the pair together. Repeat with the other Exterior rectangles. Press the seams open.

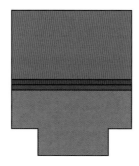

3. Position an assembled Exterior unit from Step 2 right side facing up, on a notched Fleece rectangle aligning all of the raw edges. Either quilt these units together, or baste by sewing along the raw edges. Repeat with the remaining assembled Exterior unit and the notched Fleece rectangle.

> **TIP:** *I did straight-line quilting with my walking foot, stopping just before I reached the notched corners.*

4. Fold both short edges of a Drawstring Channel by ¼" with the wrong sides together. Press and edgestitch along both folded edges. Fold along the long side with the wrong sides together, aligning the raw edges, and press again.

5. Center the assembled Drawstring unit from Step 4 along the top un-notched edge of an assembled Exterior Panel aligning the raw edges. Pin and baste into place using a ¼" seam allowance.

6. Repeat Steps 4-5 with the remaining Drawstring rectangle and Exterior Panel.

7. Box the corners using the Notched Method (see page 11) using a ³/₈" seam allowance. Be sure to carefully align the seams where the Exterior Tops and Bottom Panels meet. This will result in a continuous seam line around the bag.

ASSEMBLING THE LINING

1. Position the notched Lining rectangles, right sides together, aligning all of the raw edges. Pin in place.

2. Box the corners using a ³/₈" seam allowance, leaving approximately a 5" opening along one side for turning the bag.

3. Turn the assembled Lining right side out.

FINISHING

1. Place the assembled Lining inside the assembled Exterior, with the right sides together. Align the side seams and pin or clip along the top raw edge. Sew around the perimeter using a ³/₈" seam allowance.

2. Turn the bag out through the opening in the Lining and sew the opening closed. Push the Exterior inside the Lining with the wrong sides together.

3. Press the top edge, ensuring that the seam allowance is flat and the Drawstring Channels are positioned outside the bag. Edgestitch around the top. Turn the bag right side out.

4. Using a safety pin on one end of the cording and beginning on one side of the bag, thread the cording through both Drawstring units, tying the ends of the cording together.

5. Repeat Step 4 with the second length of cording, but this time, starting from the opposite side of the bag. This will allow the bag to be cinched closed.

BY JULIE ELLIOTT

MATERIALS

Denim: approximately 1 Fat Quarter of select pieces from old jeans

Lining: 1/3 yard quilting cotton

Lightweight fusible Interfacing: 1/3 yard

Scraps of a favorite print to appliqué and embroider

Scrap of HeatnBond Lite

Embroidery hoop, needle and floss or Perle #8 cotton

(1) 5½" x 8½", 60 page spiral sketchbook

(1) 1" button

Elastic ponytail holder with the metal closure removed if necessary

Optional: enamel pin and denim needle for your sewing machine

NOTE: *If your sketchbook is a different size, measure the height and width of the closed sketchbook (including the spiral!) and add 1" to each for the seam allowances.*

PREPARATION

1. Disassemble the jeans, identifying which elements to include on the cover. Sew the pieces together to create a rectangle approximately 16" x 10".

> **PIECING TIP:** *When creating the denim rectangle, incorporate some unique elements (original seams, waistband, pocket etc.) from your jeans.*

2. Add embroidery as desired. If adding embroidery to a pocket, embroider it first and then attach it to the right side of the front cover.

BOHO SKETCHBOOK COVER

If you're like me, your mind is constantly spinning with new ideas just waiting to be explored. My sketchbook has become the place where I record those creative nuggets and experiment with ideas. Keeping a sketchbook does require a bit of discipline, however. While the adage "Don't judge a book by its cover," may be true, I knew I needed a cover that would inspire me to pick it up regularly and encourage play. To make the cover unique to me, and for added durability, I chose to upcycle an old, well-loved pair of jeans. The front pocket houses my favorite pens and I also added embroidery to the cover itself to provide some texture.

This gift encourages someone who wants to expand his or her creativity. Consider gifting this with a coupon code for an online drawing class and let their imagination run wild.

CUTTING

From the Pieced Denim, cut:
(1) 15¼" x 9½" rectangle for the Exterior

From the Lining Fabric, cut:
(1) 15¼" x 9½" rectangle for the Lining
(2) 7" x 9½" rectangles for the Flaps

From the Interfacing, cut:
(1) 15¼" x 9½" rectangle
(2) 7" x 9½" rectangles

ASSEMBLING THE COVER

1. Fuse the HeatnBond Lite to the wrong side of the Scrap fabric. Allow to cool and fussy cut around the desired motifs printed on the fabric. Remove the paper backing and fuse to the right side of the denim Exterior.

2. Using the embroidery tools and materials, embellish as desired (see page 7 for stitches).

> **TIP:** *If you are pressed for time, attach the shapes using free-motion machine stitching.*

3. Fold the Exterior rectangle in half lengthwise and press to form a crease. Unfold the Exterior and position it right side facing up. Using the crease as a guide, position the button in the center of the right edge of the cover, approximately 1¼" away from the raw edge. Hand sew into place.

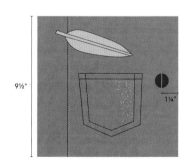

On the opposite 9½" side, align the ends of the ponytail holder along the center crease and with the ends of the holder extending slightly beyond the Exterior's raw edge. Baste in place using a ⅛" seam allowance.

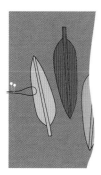

4. Fuse the 15¼" x 9½" Interfacing rectangle to the wrong side of the Lining rectangle.

5. Repeat Step 4 with the 2 remaining Interfacing and Flap rectangles.

6. Fold the Flaps in half lengthwise with the wrong sides together and press. Edgestitch along each fold.

FINISHING

1. With the Exterior, right side up, align the raw edges and position the Flaps on the 9½" sides of the Exterior.

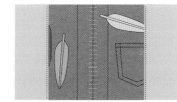

2. Position the Lining, right side down over the layered unit from Step 1, aligning the raw edges, and pin all the layers in place.

3. Sew around the cover leaving a 3" opening along the bottom for turning and being sure to backstitch at both ends.

> **TIP:** *To reinforce the corner stitching, backstitch several times in each corner.*

4. Trim the corners to reduce the bulk and turn the cover inside out. Tuck in the seam allowances of the opening from Step 3. Press and edgestitch around the entire cover. Slip the sketchbook inside of the Flaps.

CLIP CUSHION

I created the Clip Cushion because I needed a way to keep my sewing clips close and tidy. This cushion makes it easy to pick up clips and put them back so they don't get lost in the bottom of a sewing bag, or get scattered all over your sewing table. If you are like me, you like to bind your quilts in front of a favorite movie. This cushion stops the clips from falling down behind the sofa cushions and the heavy bean-bag-style filling prevents them from rolling off the arm of the couch. It's a great project to make with tiny scraps of treasured fabrics that you want to keep in your life and in your sewing box.

   Make a Clip Cushion for all of your sewing buddies in your guild (they will wonder how they ever coped without one) or add one to your swap partner's parcel as a welcome little extra.

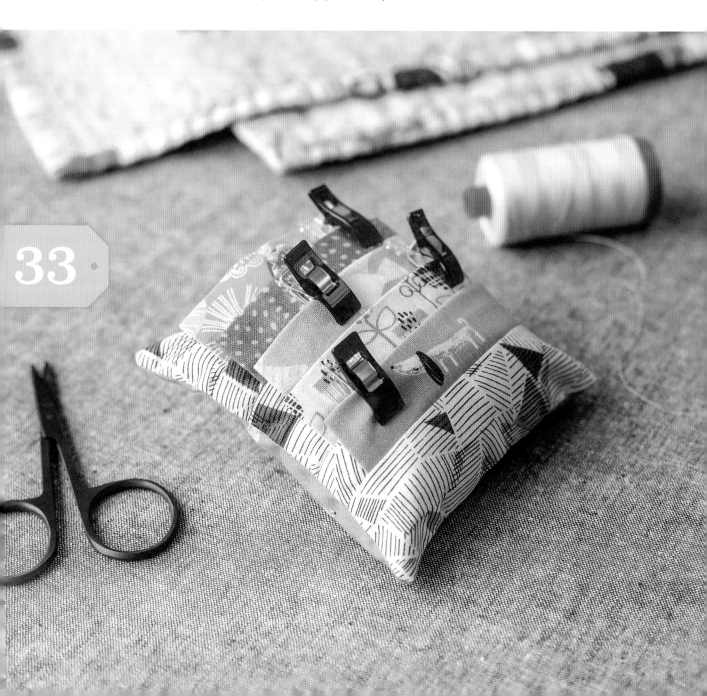

33

BY ESTHER MOOREY

. . . .

Finished Size: 4½" square

MATERIALS

A variety of scraps at least 5" wide, totaling approximately 1 Fat Eighth

Heavy filling such as rice or crushed walnut shells.

MATERIALS TIP: *The 5" width makes this perfect for using charm squares like I did!*

CUTTING

From the Scraps, cut:
(5) 4" x 2" rectangles for the Tags
(4) 5" x 1" rectangles for the Middle Strips
(2) 5" x 1¾" rectangles for the End Strips
(1) 5" square for the Backing

CUTTING TIP: *I like to fussy cut my Tags to make sure my favorite motifs sit on the front of each one.*

ASSEMBLING THE TAGS

1. Fold a Tag rectangle in half lengthwise with the right sides together. Sew across the two short ends, turn the tag right side out, and press. Repeat for the remaining 4 Tags.

2. Place an End Strip rectangle, right side up, and center an assembled Tag along the bottom edge, aligning the raw edges.

3. Arrange a Middle Strip, right side down, over the assembled unit from Step 2. Pin and sew along the bottom edge.

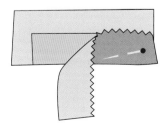

4. Finger press the seam open.

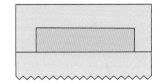

5. Repeat Steps 2-4 for the remaining Tags and Middle Strips, alternating between the two.

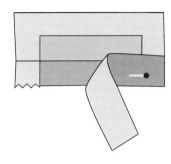

6. Finish by attaching the remaining End Strip rectangle.

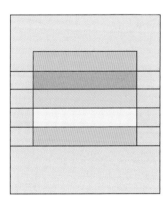

7. Press the seams lightly and trim the completed top to 5" square.

8. Position the assembled unit from Step 7 and the Backing square right sides together. Sew around the perimeter, leaving a 2" gap along the middle of one side for turning.

9. Clip the corners and turn inside out, poking them out with a chopstick or similar blunt object to get neat corners. Tuck the seam allowances into the opening and press.

10. Fill with your heavy filling so the cushion is full, but not stuffed tight.

FILLING TIP: *I use a heavy but fine grain such as rice, quinoa or cous cous as I usually have some in the cupboard. This weight means the cushion won't rise off the surface when you pull clips off the Tags. You could add a few drops of essential oils, dried lavender or cloves to your filling to scent your cushion and make it even more enjoyable to use.*

11. Whipstitch the opening from Step 8 closed and you're done!

BY MICHAEL ANN SHREEVE

Finished Size: 1" x 4"

MATERIALS

(16) 1" x 2" assorted fabric Scraps for Geese

(32) 1" x 1½" assorted fabric Scraps for the Background

(1) 1¾" x 9" Backing strip

(1) ⅞" x 9" scrap of Batting or heavy weight Interfacing

(1) 1" metal key fob hardware set

OR

(1) 1" D-ring and key ring AND

(1) 2½" x 4½" fabric Scrap for the ring attachment

HARDWARE TIPS: *I've included instructions for using either key fob Hardware or a D-ring so you can start sewing immediately and use what you have on hand! The key fob hardware will give you a bit more of a professional finish and is very quick and easy to install. D-rings may be easier to find at your local craft store and will give your keychain a sturdier finish, but do take longer to install.*

CUTTING

From the Backing Fabric, cut:
(1) 1¾" x 9" rectangle

From the Batting/Interfacing, cut:
(1) ⅞" x 9" rectangle

PAPER PIECING TIPS

· *Shorten your stitch length to about 1.5 or 12-15 stitches per inch. This will help perforate your paper for easier removal.*

· *Use a larger needle, 90/14 size.*

· *Keep a small acrylic ruler with a clear ¼" line handy.*

· *Have your iron close by!*

TINY GEESE KEYCHAIN

Do you ever finish a major sewing project only to look at your pile of scraps and think, "But they're too cute to go in the trash!"? That's how the Tiny Geese Keychain was born. This adorable, 4" long, quilty keychain is small, simple and beautifully cleans out your scrap bin. The ½" x 1" paper pieced geese uses the tiniest bits of fabric, so you can showcase those beloved small scraps you just can't bear to get rid of. I've included two hardware options, or you can use what you have on hand to finish in no time.

The Tiny Geese Keychain's small size and simple construction make it a quick and satisfying finish. The perfect gift for a new driver, homeowner or your favorite quilt shop!

PIECING THE GEESE

1. Assemble the Geese Strip using the photocopied pattern (see page 143) and paper piece the Geese (see page 93).

2. Trim around the pattern using the ¼" seam allowance line as a guide. Leave the paper attached to ensure accuracy in the next step.

ATTACHING THE BACKING

> **TIP:** *The Backing strip is ¼" wider than the assembled Geese Strip. When finished, this will create a small border on either edge of the keychain when viewed from the front.*

1. Position the Backing strip and Geese Strip with the right sides together, aligning one long edge. Using the sewing line on the paper as a guide, sew along one edge of the long seam, backstitching at both ends.

2. Line up the other long edge of the Backing Piece and Geese Strip (the backing piece will be a bit bunched, not flat). Again, using the sewing line on the paper as a guide, sew along the seam, backstitching at both ends.

FINISH THE KEYCHAIN PIECE

1. Remove the paper from the pattern. If you have difficulty removing some of the smaller pieces, try using tweezers.

2. Turn the assembled unit right side out.

> **TIP:** *Tie a piece of string about 12" long to a safety pin. Slide the safety pin through the tube and pin it to the Backing at the bottom of the tube. Gently pull on the string to pull the bottom of the tube up and inside until it comes out the top. You may need to turn it under the bottom to get it started. Continue pulling until the entire tube is right side out and unclip your safety pin.*

3. Press the assembled unit flat so there is an equal amount of Backing fabric bordering each edge of the Geese Strip.

4. Place a safety pin in the top of the Interfacing rectangle and slide it up inside the assembled unit.

> **TIP:** *It will help to slide the Interfacing from the wide end of the Geese to the pointed end, so you aren't catching the geese seam allowances. It should fit snugly between the layers.*

5. Edgestitch along both long edges.

FINISHING

1. Trim the top and bottom ends of the Keychain completely straight.

2. Using a ⅛" seam allowance, stitch along the top and bottom ends to prevent fraying.

USING THE KEY FOB HARDWARE

1. Fold the Keychain in half with the Backing together and the short ends aligned. Slide the raw edges into the key fob hardware.

2. Clamp the key fob shut (you may need to use pliers).

USING THE D-RING

1. Fold the long sides of the Attachment rectangle by ¼" with the wrong sides together and press.

2. Fold the unit from Step 1 in half, short edges and wrong sides together and press. Open and fold in each raw edge to meet at the center crease. Fold in half again enclosing all of the raw edges and press.

3. Open the Attachment rectangle and tuck in the Keychain about ¼" away from the long folded edge. Fold the Attachment rectangle back up and pin or clip in place.

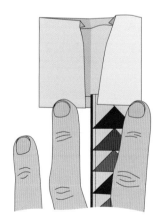

4. Slide the D-ring onto the Keychain at about the middle, so it is out of the way. Repeat Step 3 for the opposite end of the Attachment rectangle. Make sure the Keychain and Attachment rectangle form a circle without any twists. Pin or clip in place.

5. Sew the Attachment and Keychain pieces together by edgestitching all around the Attachment rectangle. Backstitch to secure the seam and position the D-ring in the center of the Attachment rectangle.

6. Fold the keychain in half, aligning the sewn ends of the Attachment rectangle.

7. Stitch together along the bottom of the Attachment rectangle, following the edge-stitching line. Because of the number of layers, you may want to use a denim needle. Carefully backstitch to secure the seam.

LITTLE TUTORIAL:
PAPER PIECING BASICS

1. To make a template, draw a 6½" square on a piece of 20 lb. paper and center a 6¼" square inside that. From the lower left corner of the inner square, draw 4 lines using Figure 1 as a reference. Number each Section 1-5. (Fig. 1)

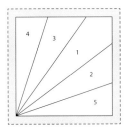

FIGURE 1

2. Cut the fabrics a little bigger than you normally would for machine piecing. Beginning with Section 1, pin your fabric to the wrong side of the template, leaving at least ½" of fabric extending past the drawn lines. The right side of the fabric should be facing up. (Fig. 2)

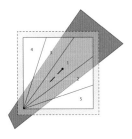

FIGURE 2

3. After ensuring your fabric selection for Section 2 also has at least ½" around all sides (hold the layers up to a sunny window to check), place the fabric for Section 2 on top of the fabric for Section 1, right sides together. Pin in place if needed. Flip over your template so that the numbers are facing you and the fabric is on the bottom.

4. Set your machine's stitch length to 1.8 mm. This will make removing the template paper a lot easier. Sew along the line between Sections 1 and 2, extending into the seam allowance.

5. Fold the paper along the sewn line so that the right sides of the paper are facing. Measure ¼" away from the sewn line onto the exposed fabric. Trim away the excess fabric and press the seams to one side.

6. Repeat for all sections of the template, working in numerical order. (Fig. 3)

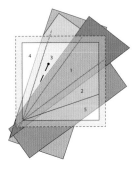

FIGURE 3

7. Press all seams again, this time on the right side of the fabric. (Fig. 4)

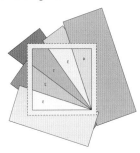

FIGURE 4

8. With the paper side facing up, trim around the template. Make sure to include the marked seam allowances around the original 6½" square drawn in Step 1. (Fig. 5)

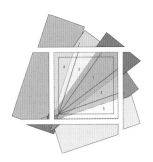

FIGURE 5

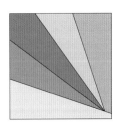

COMPLETED BLOCK

TEATIME TRAVEL CADDY

This quick and easy project is a favorite of mine. When I am on the go, I prefer to carry my own teabags, since I only drink decaf. I developed this design, using scraps of cotton fabrics and even leftovers of cotton batting from other projects. I love using scraps and you can practice your quilt-as-you-go technique too!

   This handy tea caddy makes a great gift when paired with a pretty mug and some of their favorite tea. Match your scraps to the mug colors and grab that pretty little vintage button you have been saving for just the right project.

BY LOIS JOHNSEN

....

Finished Size: 3¼" x 4½" closed

MATERIALS

Scraps of cotton fabrics for the Exterior, between ¾" – 2" wide and at least 6½" long

⅛ yard for the Lining

Scrap rectangle of Batting

(1) 3" length of ⅛" wide elastic or ponytail holder with the metal removed if necessary

(1) ½" button

Water soluble marker

CUTTING

From the Lining fabric, cut:
(3) 5" x 7" rectangles

From the Batting, cut:
(1) 6" x 8" rectangle

ASSEMBLING THE EXTERIOR

1. Arrange the random Scraps of fabric in a pleasing manner to piece the Exterior rectangle.

2. Draw a vertical line toward the center of the 6"x 8" Batting, and position the first fabric Scrap right side facing up on the marked line.

3. Position the next Scrap, right sides together and aligning the raw edges and stitch.

4. Open the seam and press the second strip into place.

5. Attach a third Scrap to the left of first strip, right sides together and aligning the raw edges.

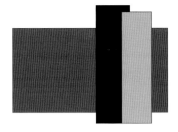

6. Continue adding Strips to the Batting, pressing as you go, until the Batting is covered.

> **TIP:** *This is the perfect place to utilize the decorative stitches on your sewing machine. Stitch each seam with fancy stitches and fun threads or decorate each strip.*

7. Trim the assembled unit from Step 6 to a 5" x 7" rectangle.

ASSEMBLING THE LINING

1. Fold a 5" x 7" Lining rectangle in half with the long edges and wrong sides together, and press. Edgestitch along the fold. Repeat with a second Lining rectangle.

2. On the right side of the 7" edge of the remaining 5" x 7" Lining rectangle, mark a line 1⅝" from the top raw edge. Position the folded edge of an assembled Pocket from Step 1 along the drawn line and pin in place. Stitch ¼" away from the bottom raw edge.

3. Arrange the second assembled Pocket from Step 1 on top of the assembled unit from Step 2, aligning the raw edges. Pin in place. Baste along the sides and across the bottom close to the edges, securing both pocket sides.

4. Fold the assembled unit in half, short edges together and press to form a crease. Starting at the bottom of the unit, stitch along the crease to the top of the Pockets, backstitching at the top edge.

5. Fold the elastic in half to form a loop. Using a ⅛" seam allowance, baste the elastic to the right side of the assembled Lining just above the lower Pocket folded edge and aligning the raw edges.

> **TIP:** *Hair elastics from the bargain store are perfect for using on projects like this one. They come in lots of fun colors and are very inexpensive.*

FINISHING

1. Position the pieced Exterior and the assembled Lining right sides together and pin.

2. Stitch around the perimeter leaving a 3" opening along the bottom for turning. Trim the corners, being careful not to cut through the stitching. Turn the caddy right side out.

3. Tuck in the seam allowance with the wrong sides together and press well. Edgestitch around the perimeter closing the opening from Step 2.

4. Close the caddy and using the edge of the Elastic loop as a guide, hand sew the Button in place, being careful to stitch through only the Exterior and Batting.

BY DEONN STOTT

Finished Size: 1½" x 2½"

MATERIALS

Main Body Fabric: 2½" x 5" rectangle

Accent Fabric: 5" square

Yellow Beak Fabric: 1½" square

Filler (poly fiberfill, wool roving, silica sand, rice, ground walnut shells, lavender leaves, all work well)

Washable glue stick

Miniature elastic band

(1) 1½" button (optional for pincushion)

(1) 8" length of narrow ribbon (optional for ornament or sachet)

CUTTING

From the Accent Fabric, cut:
(1) 1½" x 5" rectangle
(1) 1" x 5" rectangle
(2) 2½" squares

NOTE: *The instructions given here are for creating one bird.*

ASSEMBLING THE BIRD

1. Fold the 1½" Yellow square in half and press. Bring the folded corners to the center, forming a triangle (prairie point); press again. Fold in half again to form a pointy little Beak.

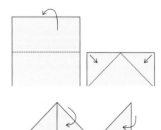

2. Repeat Step 1 with each of the 2½" Accent squares for the Wings.

LITTLE BIRD PINCUSHION

These sweet little birds always make me smile. A student in a class I taught gave me a similar little birdie and I fell in love! They are so easy to make using a couple of 5" squares, a tiny scrap for the beak, and about 2 Tablespoons of filler-that's it! Add a ribbon to turn it into an ornament. Or gift a flock and use a few drops of essential oil on the filler for a sachet to keep their closet smelling nice. Do you have a favorite charm pack just waiting to be turned into a new project? This is an ideal project to showcase those co-ordinated fabrics. Whether you make one or make a ton, it's the sweetest little gift!

3. Arrange the assembled Wings along one edge of the Main 2½" x 5" rectangle, ½" from the outer edges, leaving about 1½" of space between the Wings. Pin or glue-baste in place.

4. Position the 1½" wide Accent fabric rectangle along the Wing edge of the assembled Main rectangle. Position the 1" wide Accent fabric rectangle along the opposite edge, with the right sides together and aligning the raw edges. Stitch together and press the seams open.

5. With the wrong side still facing up, fold a long edge of the 1" wide Accent fabric rectangle by ¼" and press to form a crease. Unfold.

6. Fold the assembled unit from Step 5 in half, short edges and right sides together. Align the side seams and pin. Insert the closed folded edge of the Beak near the fold of the 1½" Accent Fabric rectangle. Pin the Beak in place.

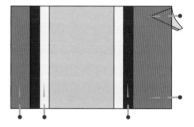

7. Backstitching at the beginning and end, stitch along the Beak edge, to secure in place. Pivot at the corner and stitch along the bottom, leaving the seam opposite the Beak open.

8. With the wrong side still out, flatten the unit by centering the long seam. On the edge opposite the Beak, finger press the seams open and pin, matching the seams. Stitch a straight line along the edge of the seam allowance, about ¾" from the

tip. This will box the corner and form the little bird's Body. No need to trim the seam.

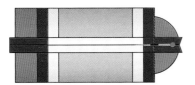

> **TIP:** *Tuck the Beak section down inside the tube of the Body to make it easier to sew the box seam.*

9. Turn the assembled unit right side out and fill the bird head and only about half of the Body with your choice of stuffing; about 2 Tablespoons of Filler.

10. Re-fold the raw edges of the Tail along the pressed lines from Step 5. Center the seam and

pin the folded edges together. Stitch by hand or edgestitch to close the opening at the Tail.

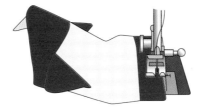

> **TIP:** *Shake the filler down toward the head as far as it will go and secure with a pin while stitching the final seam.*

11. Hold the bird with the Beak side down and shake any filler out of the Tail area. Use a mini elastic band and wrap it around as many times as possible to cinch in the Body and form the Tail. Fan out the Tail.

If you prefer, take a running stitch all the way around the Body center about ¼" away from the stuffing, then tighten to gather. Wrap the thread around several times and secure with a knot, then bury the threads.

FINISHING

Add eyes by stitching tiny buttons, seed beads, or French knots (see page 7) or simply use pins. Lastly, give a little tug on the Beak to straighten it out.

For a sachet, use the ribbon and follow the instructions from Abby on her Pickle Ornament (see page 42) for attaching.

For a pincushion, glue a large button to the bottom of the bird as a base and load your new pincushion with pins, if you can bear to poke him!

BY CHASE WU

Finished Size: 8" x 5½"

MATERIALS

Main (a linen/cotton blend):
1 Fat Quarter

Clear Vinyl: ¼ yard

Binding: ¼ yard

Medium weight fusible Interfacing: ¼ yard

(1) 10" nylon zipper

Water soluble marker

CUTTING

From the Main Fabric, cut:
(4) 1½" x 3" rectangles
(4) 1½" x 8" rectangles
(2) 5½" x 8" rectangles

From the Interfacing, cut:
(4) 1" x 2½" rectangles
(4) 1" x 7½" rectangles
(2) 5" x 7½" rectangles

From the Vinyl, cut:
(1) 3" x 6" rectangle

From the Binding Fabric, cut:
(1) 1¾" x WOF strip

ASSEMBLING THE EXTERIOR

1. Fuse the Interfacing to the wrong side of the Main fabric rectangles leaving ¼" of Main fabric exposed around the perimeter of the Interfacing.

2. Position (2) 1½" x 3" Main rectangles right sides together. Insert the 3" edge of the Vinyl rectangle between them, aligning the raw edges and stitch. Position the Main rectangles wrong sides together and gently finger press along the sewn seam. Topstitch to secure the sewn edges.

WINDOW ZIPPERED POUCH

Every year before school starts, we've always enjoyed shopping for school supplies. One year we were looking for the ring binder pencil case, but nothing caught my daughter's eye. She asked me, if I'd be able to make one instead. A week after making hers, I modified my pattern into this small window zippered pouch.

Stitch one up as a hand-sewing project bag, as a gift for your favorite toddler who enjoys collecting 'things', or use it as I have—as a first aid kit! Load it with fresh supplies like bandages, antibacterial ointment, tweezers for those surprise splinters and a travel-size tube of sunscreen. Throw in a lollipop or some stickers if you are gifting this to someone with little ones (every patient deserves a treat!).

3. Repeat Step 2 along the opposite short edge of the Vinyl and, using the (4) 1½"x 8" rectangles, along the long edges of the Vinyl. This creates the Main Exterior Front and the Main Lining Front.

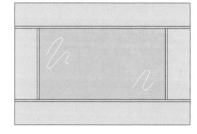

4. Fold back one long Lining rectangle. Position the zipper along the 8" edge of just the Main Exterior Front, right sides together. With the zipper pull at the left, align the raw edges and sew the zipper to the 8" edge. Take care not to sew through the Lining. Fold the raw edge of the zipper inside the top Main Exterior Front rectangle by ¼". Carefully press along the zipper seam using a warm iron setting and avoiding the Vinyl. Edgestitch along the fold of the Exterior, again avoiding the Lining.

5. On the opposite Main Lining Front rectangle without the zipper, fold the 8" raw edge by ¼" to the wrong side and press.

6. With the Lining facing up, align the top Main and Lining rectangles with the wrong sides together. With the zipper tape in between, enclosing all of the raw edges, sew all three layers together slightly to one side of the topstitching from Step 4.

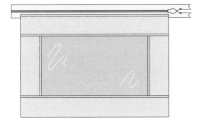

7. Position the remaining (2) 5½" x 8" Main rectangles wrong sides together. Layer the assembled panel from Step 6 with the Exterior facing up. Align the raw edges and pin. Using a ⅛" seam allowance, baste around the perimeter, being sure to open up the zipper before sewing.

8. Trim away the excess zipper tape ends and attach the Binding using your favorite method.

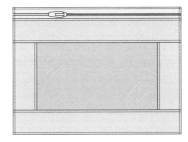

TIP: *Before sewing two ends of the Binding together, gently fold the Pouch in half. This will make it easier to join your Binding ends.*

LITTLE TUTORIAL: BINDING STRIPS

1. Fold the Binding strip in half lengthwise, aligning the raw edges and press to create a crease. Open up the strip and bring the two long raw edges of the strip to the center, using the crease as a guide. Refold along the center crease, enclosing the long raw edges and press again.

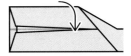

TIP: *Modify the length of the Main and Interfacing rectangles to create a 13" square with a large 11" vinyl window for a quilt block project bag.*

37

BY SUSANNE WOODS

Finished Size: 10" x 20"
(sizes may vary)

MATERIALS

Variety of Scraps for the Patchwork Layer

Main: 1 Fat Quarter

Backing: 1 Fat Quarter

Binding: 1 Fat Quarter

Batting: 10" x 20" rectangle

20# paper

Water soluble marker

CUTTING

From both the Main and Backing Fabrics, cut:
(1) 10" x 20" rectangle

From the Binding Fabric, cut:
(2) 2½" x WOF strips

PREPARATION

1. Select a word or number. Use the number of digits or letters in your word/number to calculate the width of each Patchwork Panel. For example, if there are four numbers, each Patchwork Panel will be 5" wide finished resulting in a 20" wide mini. If there are six numbers, consider adjusting the total finished width to 24" so that each pieced panel will finish at 4" wide.

2. Trace or photocopy the appropriate numbers onto a sheet or two of 20# copy paper. Select a font size that is at least 2" shorter and narrower than the height and width of each Patchwork Panel determined in Step 1. For example, in my version using three numbers, my patchwork panels are 7" wide and 11" high and my numbers are 5" wide x 7" high.

HOUSE NUMBER MINI

I learned this raw edge reverse appliqué technique from Dan Rouse during his Mighty Lucky Quilting Club challenge. I created a mini of our house number to hang outside the covered porch of our front door. Since walls of mini quilts seem to be all the rage these days, I'm going to make a house number for each address we have lived in, as our next anniversary gift to my husband (shhhhh!). Dan's technique is really cathartic. By using your favorite scraps as the background piecing, you never know which ones will be revealed when you cut away your top layer. Kind of like life (and marriage!)—you can't guarantee the exact outcome, but the results are beautifully unexpected.

These minis make thoughtful anniversary, baby shower, housewarming or teacher gifts (think room numbers!). Does your swap partner choose a word every year to remind him of what he wants to focus on in the coming 12 months? Consider using text instead of numbers to piece an inspirational word or a child's name to hang outside their bedroom door. Just be sure to select a nice chunky font to make the cutting away of the top layer easier and to ensure your results are legible from a distance.

3. Cut out the numbers from the paper to use as templates.

> **TIP:** *You want the Patchwork Panels to finish around 1" higher than the 10" high Main rectangle so that you can see where each Patchwork Panel ends when positioning your number templates.*

PIECING THE PATCHWORK PANELS

1. Improv piece (or use a series of 2" squares if preferred) the appropriate number of Patchwork Panels each using a different color of scraps and finishing at least 11" high.

> **TIP:** *Make sure you have the appropriate permissions to use the fonts of your choice.*

2. Sew together the assembled Patchwork Panels along the long side and press.

3. Trim to 11" x 21" if necessary.

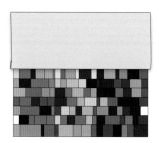

38

ASSEMBLING THE MINI

1. Position the assembled Patchwork unit onto the Batting, right side facing up. Layer the Main rectangle over the Patchwork unit, also right side facing up and centering on the Patchwork unit. There should be approximately ½" of each Patchwork Panel visible on the top and bottom of your layered mini. Pin in place.

2. Place the number templates in order on the Main rectangle, using the exposed Patchwork seams as a guide to ensure each number will not cross over into another colored Patchwork Panel.

3. Using a water soluble marker, trace around each number.

4. Using the drawn lines from Step 3 as a guide, stitch around each number twice through all the layers.

TIP: *If you'd like to add more texture, consider going around each number a few times to build up that thread texture.*

5. Being careful to only cut away the Main fabric, trim inside the stitch line leaving approximately ¼" of fabric revealing the Patchwork Panels in the shape of the numbers.

6. Clip the inside corners if necessary to encourage fraying.

7. If additional quilting is desired, add that now. Trim the quilted mini to 10" x 20".

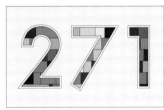

FINISHING

1. Create the Binding Strips (see page 99). Position the assembled Exterior on the Backing rectangle, wrong sides together, and attach the Binding using your favorite method.

2. Put the completed mini in the washing machine and dryer to encourage fraying of the raw edges.

TIP: *For hanging, add a mini sleeve at the back or attach a pretty piece of ribbon to the top prior to binding.*

BY RANA HEREDIA

Finished Size: 2" tall

MATERIALS

(2) 5" squares for the Body

(3) 5" squares for the Shell

1 yard of embroidery floss

2 straight pins

(1) ¾" button

Ground walnut shells or filling

Doll-maker's needle

Perle #8 cotton

Freezer paper

CUTTING

Create two freezer paper templates from the Snail patterns (see page 135).

From the Body Fabric, cut:
(2) Body units using the freezer paper (do not add a seam allowance)

From the Shell Fabric, cut:
(3) Shell units using the freezer paper (do not add a seam allowance)

ASSEMBLING THE SHELL

1. Position 2 of the Shell units right sides together. Sew along one long side of the wedges.

2. Open the 2 pieces and position the third wedge, right sides together. Starting at the bottom, sew along one side until you reach the seam allowance at the top. Leaving the needle down, pivot the piece and sew down the other side.

ESCARGOT PINCUSHION

Finally! A snail that you are actually going to want to have around the house. If you are a button collector, this is a project worthy of one your prettiest buttons to sit on his shell. Because the pattern calls for 5" squares, this is a charm-pack-friendly pincushion and really shows off those large scale patterns well, despite the small size. Make a few to gift to all of your sewing guild-mates. It just can't get any cuter than this little guy.

3. Trim the seam allowance at the point to ⅛" and turn right side out.

4. Use your fingers to turn the raw edge under about ⅛". Baste around the opening with a good, strong thread leaving a 5" tail of thread for gathering.

TIP: *Ground walnut shells can be found at the pet shop. If you prefer a different stuffing, go for it!*

5. Using a small funnel, add about 3 tablespoons of walnut shells. Leave about ½" of headspace. Do not overfill.

6. Pull the thread to gather the opening closed. Adjust the amount of filling, if needed.

7. Stitch the opening closed using the same thread.

8. Using about 30" of Perle cotton and the doll-maker's needle, pull the thread through the Shell starting at the bottom and going out at the top.

9. Wrap the thread down the side of the Shell, covering a seam. Bring the needle down through the bottom again. Repeat until every seam is covered. End with the floss at the top, but do not cut it yet.

ASSEMBLING THE BODY

1. Position the 2 Body units right sides facing. Stitch together leaving the bottom open.

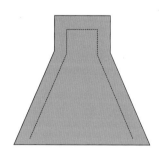

2. Clip the top corners and notch the seam allowance along both sides at the "neck" and turn the Body right side out.

3. Repeat Steps 6-7 of Assembling the Shell, gently shaping the Body by manipulating it with your fingers. You want to make a stubby 'L' shape

so that there is a place for the Shell to sit. Work it so that the gathered hole on the bottom migrates toward the back end so that it won't be seen.

FINISHING

1. Position the assembled Shell onto the bottom portion of the stubby 'L' shaped Body.

2. Making sure the needle will go through the holes, position the button on top of the Shell and run the needle and thread through it and then down through the Shell and the Body. Pull the threads snuggly to secure. Repeat a few times until all of the units are secure.

3. Knot and cut the thread.

4. Finish by adding 2 Pins to the head. You may want to bend them slightly. Or not!

TIP: *There will be a small gap between the neck/head of the snail and the Shell. If you want to minimize the gap for a more upright snail, apply a small dab of hot glue to the back of the head/neck and gently press it into the Shell holding it in place until the glue hardens.*

39

BY HEIDI STAPLES

....

Finished Size: 2" x 3" x 4½"

MATERIALS

Main: 10" square

Trim: 10" square

Lining: 10" square

Fusible Batting: 10" square

Muslin: 10" square

(1) 5" length of 1" wide twill tape

Adhesive basting spray

Water soluble marker

CUTTING

From the Main Fabric, cut:
(2) 3¼" x 8" rectangles

From the Trim Fabric, cut:
(2) 1¼" x 8" rectangles

From the Lining, Muslin and Batting, cut:
(2) 4" x 8" rectangles

From the twill tape, cut:
(2) 2½" long rectangles

ASSEMBLING THE BASKET

1. Position a Main and Trim rectangle with the right sides together, and stitch along the long edge. Press the seam open. Fuse a Batting rectangle to the wrong side of the assembled unit and quilt as desired. (I simply topstitched a line ⅛" above the seam on the Trim rectangle.) Repeat with the remaining Main, Trim and Batting rectangles.

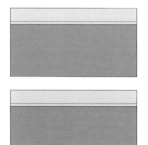

PIXIE BASKET

This little basket represents everything that I love in a sewing project. It's quick to sew, pretty to look at, and surprisingly useful. The Pixie Basket makes a fantastic last-minute gift that can be filled with all sorts of items to personalize it for the recipient: mini charm packs, spools of thread, binding clips, candy, paper clips, crayons, nail polish, or any other small item that strikes your fancy. You can easily sew one of these in an hour or less, and it's a fun way to feature several favorite prints on an item that will be used every day.

2. Clip or pin the assembled panels from Step 1 with the right sides together and aligning all the raw edges. Sew all around both 4" sides and the bottom, leaving the top Trim edge open, and backstitching at the start and finish of the seam. Press the seams open.

3. Position the assembled unit from Step 2 into a square with the wrong sides facing up, and the side seam allowances aligned. Using a water soluble marker and a ruler, mark a line from one folded edge to another, parallel to the long raw edges and 3" in length. Repeat for the opposite corner, ensuring that the length of each line is identical before stitching along the marked lines.

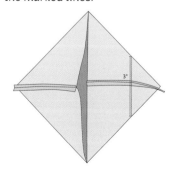

4. Trim away the excess fabric ¼" away from the outside edge of the stitching from Step 3. Repeat for the opposite corner.

5. Turn the basket right side out and push out the corners using a blunt object. Fold a piece of twill tape in half so that the short ends meet. Baste the raw ends together to form a loop. Center the folded twill tape along a side seam of the assembled Exterior, aligning the raw edges. Using a ⅛" seam allowance, baste in place on the Exterior. Repeat with the remaining piece of twill tape on the other side seam.

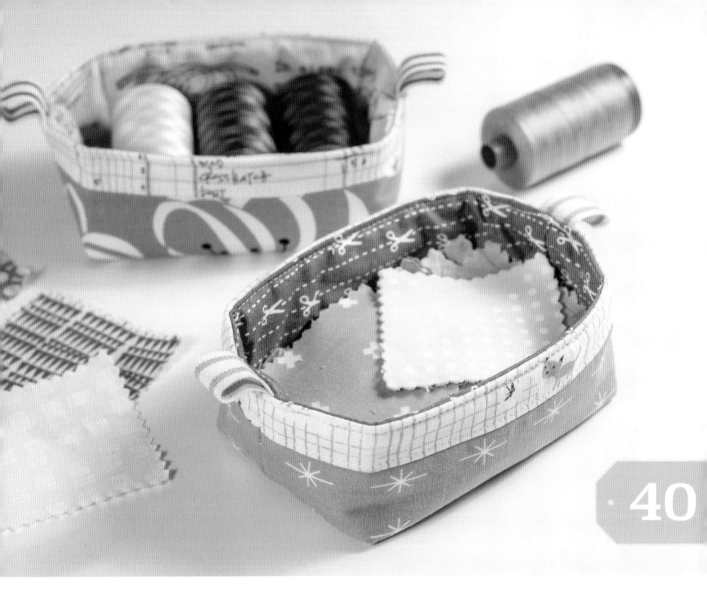

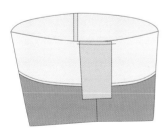

6. Using the adhesive basting spray, fuse a Lining and Muslin rectangle together, wrong sides together. Repeat with the remaining Lining and Muslin rectangles. Repeat Steps 2-4 to form the basket Lining.

TIP: *When using basting spray, follow the manufacturer's instructions. Be sure to wear a mask and work in a well ventilated area or outdoors.*

7. Position the Exterior inside the Lining with the right sides together and clip or pin around the top opening, aligning the side seams. Stitch around the perimeter leaving a 3" opening for turning. Press the seam allowance open, including at the opening. This pressing will result in a crisp finish when the project is turned right side out.

8. Pull the basket right side out through the opening, push the Lining into the basket, tuck in the seam allowance around the opening and press the entire basket carefully.

9. Edgestitch around the top of the basket, closing the opening as you stitch.

TIP: *To give your basket a boxy shape, press all the creases at the corners and edges until they are sharp rather than rounded.*

BY JULES MCMAHON

Finished Size: 12½" x 16"

MATERIALS

Exterior: ½ yard

Non-directional Lining: ½ yard

Pocket: 1 Fat Quarter (optional)

4 yards of ¼-½" cording

Large safety pin

Water soluble marker

(1) 9" zipper & zipper foot (optional)

(2) ½" grommets & grommet tool

CUTTING

From the Exterior Fabric, cut:
(2) 14" x 16" rectangles
From the Lining Fabric, cut:
(2) 14" x 18" rectangles
From the cording, cut:
(2) 2 yard lengths

Optional Pocket Fabric, cut:
(1) 10" x 16" rectangle
(1) 10" x 3" rectangle
(2) 1" x 3" rectangles

A ½" seam allowance is used throughout unless otherwise stated.

THE OPTIONAL POCKET

1. Create and attach two zipper Tabs to the zipper using the instructions from the Signature Basic Bag (see page 8) and trim to 10" long.

2. Align the zipper with one short edge of the 10" x 16" rectangle, right sides together. Pin and stitch along the 10" side using a zipper foot. Press. Repeat with the 10" x 3" rectangle along the opposite side of the zipper tape.

3. With the zipper open halfway, fold the Pocket in half along the 16" length. Align the raw edges and pin the sides. Sew around three raw edges using a ¼" seam

KNITTING (AND A HUNDRED OTHER USES) BAG

This bag is a favorite of mine for so many reasons, mostly though because it's versatile and quick to make! When I was first knitting, I would carry around my knitting in my purse and it would turn into a hot mess. Then I started putting it in a zipper pouch but I found that firstly, I wanted to be able to keep my yarn in the pouch as I knitted without it snagging on zipper teeth and secondly, the pouches were just too small.

It's super-handy for carrying knitting projects as it's big enough to fit a decent sized project. I also use these bags for EPP quilt projects, taking my lunch to the office, children's library bags and a myriad of other things. You could easily make this a swimming bag or a cloth diaper bag by leaving out the pocket and lining it with a laminated fabric for water resistance.

allowance. Turn the Pocket right side out through the open zipper and press. Topstitch along three edges leaving the top unsewn.

4. Center the Pocket along a 14" edge of a Lining rectangle. Be sure that the unsewn edge of the Pocket is at the top edge of the Lining. Baste along the top edge of the Pocket.

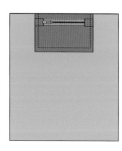

ASSEMBLING THE BAG

1. Position an Exterior and Lining rectangle right sides together. Align the short edges. Pin, stitch together, then press the seams toward the Exterior.

Repeat with the other Exterior and Lining rectangles.

2. Position the two assembled panels from Step 1 right sides together and pin. The two Exteriors should be facing and the two Linings also facing.

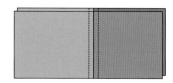

3. Use pins on each long side of the Lining to mark a 1" gap, ½" away from the seam that joins the Lining to the Exterior on each side of the bag – this will form the Casing openings. Stitch around the perimeter leaving the 1" gaps for the Casing and a 5" opening in the Lining for turning. Clip the corners.

4. Turn the Lining in at the openings to match the seam allowances. At the Casing gaps, hand stitch these 1" folds and press.

5. Turn the bag right side out. The Lining should extend above the Exterior by 1". Press the whole bag so it lays flat.

6. Edgestitch around the top of the bag on the Lining. Repeat on the Exterior just below the Lining and Exterior seam. This encloses the Casing for the Cording.

7. Hand or machine stitch the opening in the Lining from Step 3 closed.

INSTALLING THE GROMMETS

1. At the bottom corners of the bag, sew a few tacking stitches to hold the layers together. Using a water soluble marker, mark 2" away from each bottom corner edge.

2. Using a grommet tool, and following the manufacturer's instructions, install a grommet in the two bottom corners using the mark from Step 1 as a guide for centering the holes.

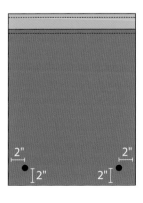

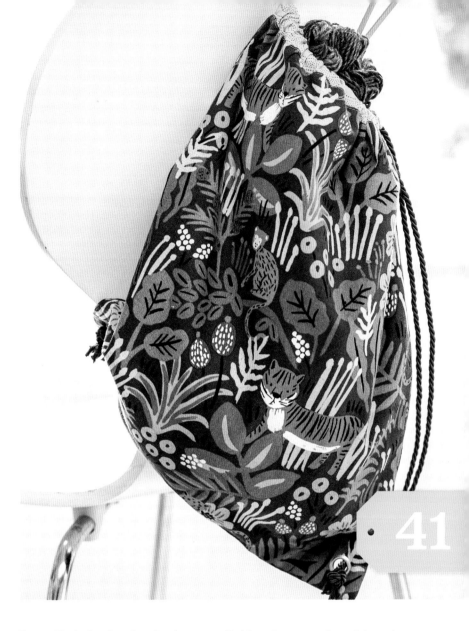

41

TIP: Find a hard surface (such as concrete) to hammer on when creating the holes using the grommet tool — a table will absorb too much shock preventing the punch from going through of all of the fabric the layers.

INSTALLING THE CORDING

1. Attach a safety pin to one end of a length of cording. Thread the cording through the Casing opening, pulling it out through the same opening.

2. Align the two ends and thread both through the grommet on the same side of the bag as the Casing opening from Step 1. Knot the ends together. If you decide not to use a grommet, simply knot the ends together and trim.

3. Repeat Steps 1 and 2 with the second length of cording on the other side of the bag.

42

BY SUSANNE WOODS

Finished Size: 10" x 13"

MATERIALS

Background/Backing:
1 Fat Quarter

Circle: 1 Fat Quarter

Binding: ⅛ yard

Batting: 11" x 14"

Double-sided fusible Interfacing: ⅛ yard

Selvage strip (optional)

CUTTING

From the Background/Backing Fabric, cut:
(2) 11" x 14" rectangles

From the Circle Fabric, cut:
(2) 6" squares

From the Binding Fabric, cut:
(1) 2½" x WOF strip

From the Interfacing cut:
(2) 6" squares

PET'S MEALTIME MAT

Welcoming a new tiny (and furry!) member of the family? Create a special Pet Food Mat just for them. We keep our feeding area in the kitchen, so when we brought home our cat from the SPCA, I wanted to make a mat that would match our décor and her personality. Since feeding her is the kids' job, I used fabrics that they would enjoy too.

This is definitely a one-hour-make with easy raw edge appliqué, but if you prefer to appliqué by hand, go for it! With so many pet-themed novelty fabrics available, you will have a blast selecting just the right one for your favorite fuzzy friend.

ASSEMBLING THE MAT

1. Fuse the Interfacing to the wrong side of the 6" Circle squares. Using the pattern (see page 139), cut a 5" circle from each.

2. Fold a Background/Backing rectangle in half both length-wise and widthwise and press to form two creases. Fold the Circles in half and finger press.

3. Unfold all three and using the creases from Step 2 for guidance, position the Circles on the Background rectangle, approximately 1" away from the vertical center. Fuse into place.

4. On a flat surface, place the Backing rectangle wrong side up. Layer the Batting rectangle on top. Position the assembled unit from Step 3 onto the Batting rectangle, right side facing up and aligning the raw edges. Pin the layers together.

5. Using a narrow zig zag stitch setting on your machine, attach the circles around the raw edges through all of the layers.

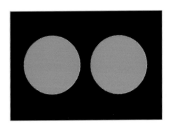

TIP: *If you would like to add additional quilting, do so at this step. If one of your fabrics has a cute selvage edge like mine did, cut to the desired length + ½", fold in each of the short ends in by ¼" and press. Position the selvage where desired on the Background fabric, aligning the raw edges (remember the selvage edge won't fray!) and pin.*

6. Trim the mat to 10" x 13" and attach the Binding using your favorite method.

43

BY GIOIA VALDEMARCA

MATERIALS AND CUTTING FOR THE BRAIDED VERSION

(3) 1½" x 15" Strips cut on the bias

4" long chain (or longer, as you prefer. You can buy it longer and shorten it later).

MATERIALS FOR THE WOVEN VERSION

(4-5) 1½" x 15" Strips

3 decorative rings (optional)

MATERIALS FOR BOTH

Hand-sewing needle

1 clasp

2 connectors

Strong glue

Pliers

BRAIDED NECKLACE

Here is a project to make a braided necklace two ways. It's a perfect, pretty, last-minute gift and a great way to use up fabric scraps or showcases your (or a friend's) latest favorite fabric. I had a lot of fun choosing the color palettes for my versions, which are made using two Fat Quarters from Kaffe Fassett. Since this project doesn't require a lot of fabric, and it will be touching the skin, try adding luscious wool or soft and light silk. Add some bling by hand sewing a few small beads to the finished piece. Want a coordinating item? Just shorten the fabric strips and you'll have a bracelet version! Your local craft store should have all of the materials you will need in their jewelry-making section, or check out Etsy for some beautiful and unique connectors.

ASSEMBLING THE NECKLACE

1. Following the instructions on page 99, create binding strips from each fabric Strip, and edgestitch along the open folded edge.

2. Position the short raw edge of your Strips one on top of the other, and hand-sew them together approximately ⅛" from the edge.

> **TIP:** If making the Braided version (inset, facing page), position 2 of the strips at opposite 45-degree angles to make braiding easier.

3. Braid your Strips together creating a tighter, shorter flat assembled unit if making the Braided version and a looser, longer assembled unit if making the Woven version (main photograph, facing page).

4. Repeat Step 2 for the remaining Strip short edges.

5. Use a few drops of the strong glue on one sewn end and insert into a connector.

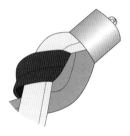

6. On the opposite sewn end, string on the three decorative rings if using and repeat Step 5.

7. After the glue has dried, use the pliers to attach a ring to the connector and then the chain to the ring.

8. Adjust the chain to the desired length, then attach the ring and the chain to the remaining connector.

44

BY KARI VOJTECHOVSKY

....

Finished Size: 24" diameter (plus the pom poms)

MATERIALS

A variety of Accent Fabrics: ¼ yard each or 16 scraps at least 6" x 7"

Backing Fabric: ¾ yard

Batting: at least 26" square

(8) 2½" pom poms (see the Little Tutorial on page 115)

Template plastic

Adhesive basting spray

PREPARATION AND CUTTING

Trace the Good Times Triangle pattern (see page 130) onto the template plastic and cut out.

From the Assorted Accent Fabrics, cut:
16 Triangles using the template

From each of the Backing Fabric and Batting, cut:
(1) 26" square

ASSEMBLING THE EXTERIOR

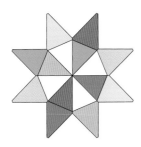

1. Using the illustration above as a reference, arrange the 16 Triangles into a pleasing color arrangement.

2. Position 2 Triangles, right sides together, aligning the short sides and stitch. Press the seam open. Repeat to make a total of 8 Triangle Pairs.

GOOD TIMES CAKE STAND PARTY MAT

This unique table topper is a happy addition to any celebration! From birthdays to holidays to baby showers, just add a cake on a stand for an instant centerpiece. I've used solids on mine with the intention of being able to reuse the topper for various occasions. But it can also be made with prints to go with a specific event or theme. With the festive pom poms, you can even paper piece the outer triangles into party hats! The construction goes together quickly with the easy-to-align templates and no binding.

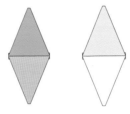

TIP: *I normally advocate pressing the seams to the side to increase the strength in a quilt top. But you need to press the seams open on this mat to reduce the seam bulk for ease of construction.*

3. Position 2 Triangle Pairs right sides together, aligning the center seams from Step 2. Stitch along one long edge. Press the seam open. Repeat with the remaining Triangle Pairs, always sewing along the same long edge of the two pieces.

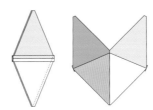

4. Position 2 units from Step 3 right sides together, aligning the center seams from Step 2. Stitch along the long edge to create half of the star shape. Press the seam open. Repeat to make the second half of the topper.

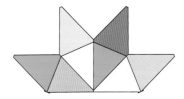

5. With the right sides together, sew the topper halves from Step 4 together to complete the Exterior. Press the seam open.

FINISHING

1. Lightly spray baste the Batting square to the wrong side of the Backing square.

TIP: *When using basting spray, follow the manufacturer's instructions. Be sure to wear a mask and work in a well ventilated area or outside.*

2. On the wrong side, use a pencil to mark an opening for turning along one edge of an outer triangle. One mark should be 1" from the tip of a triangle and another at 1" from a seam in the inner corner.

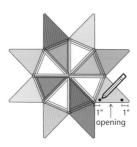

3. With the Backing square right side up on the Batting square, position the Exterior on the Backing square with the right sides together and pin in place.

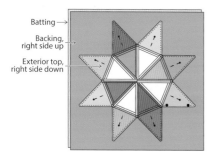

4. Backstitching at the starting and stopping points, begin stitching at one mark from Step 2. Stitch around the perimeter until you reach the second mark.

TIP: *In the inside corners, pivot at the point where the seams meet.*

5. Trim the Batting and Backing fabric at the edge of the Exterior. Carefully trim the Batting from the seam allowance and the fabric from the points, leaving approximately a ⅛" seam allowance. Be careful not to clip the fabric or stitches.

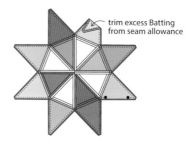

trim excess Batting from seam allowance

6. At the inside corners, clip the Backing fabric to within 3–4 threads from the pivot point. Rip the stitches to the pivot point on the inside corners of the top.

7. Turn right side out through the opening from Step 4. Use a chopstick or similar blunt object to push out the points. Press.

8. Tuck in the seam allowance from the opening and press well. Edgestitch around the perimeter, closing the opening at the same time.

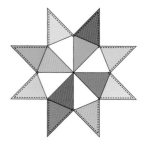

9. If desired, create the 8 yarn pom poms (see the Making Pom Poms Tutorial, facing).

10. Quilt as desired and, if using, attach the pom poms by hand to finish.

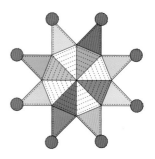

LITTLE TUTORIAL:
MAKING YARN POM POMS

MATERIALS

1 skein of worsted weight yarn

Cardboard & scissors

PREPARATION

Photocopy the pom pom pattern (see page 130) onto 20# paper

> **NOTE:** *For a quick alternative to making the pom poms, use the Clover Large pom pom Maker in the 2½" size.*

1. Cut 2 pom pom disk templates out of cardboard or heavy-weight chipboard.

2. Put both disks together. Wrap yarn around the templates very densely but not too tightly. The more yarn you use, the fluffier your pom pom will be.

The yarn should be at least as dense as shown in the photograph below.

3. Cut the yarn along the outer edge with your scissors between the two cardboard disks, carefully keeping the cut yarn from falling through the center.

4. Take a new 18" length of yarn and tie it around the cut yarn between the two cardboard disks, tightly tying all the cut yarn together and knotting. Repeat 2–3 times to secure the pom pom.

5. Remove the cardboard disks. Give a gentle tug to your pom pom. If any of the yarn seems loose, take a threaded needle and sew through the center of the pom pom several times at different angles until all the yarn is firmly attached. Snip off the excess yarn tails and fluff to shape. If needed, trim to even out your pom pom.

BY SHERRI SYLVESTER

Finished Size: 8" x 5½"

MATERIALS/CUTTING

Large Feature Print Scrap
See Exterior cutting below

From the Main Fabric, cut:
(1) Exterior Back
(2) Exterior Sides (mirrored)
(2) 1¾" x 8¾" rectangles for the Zipper sides
(1) 4" x 2" rectangle for the Zipper Tabs

From the Lining Fabric, cut:
(2) Linings

From ¼ yard of medium weight fusible Interfacing, cut:
(2) Exterior Backs
(2) 1⅜" x 8¾" rectangles for the Zipper Sides
(1) 4" x 2" rectangle for Tabs

(1) 9" nylon zipper

Water soluble marker

Pinking shears

(1) 3" length of ¼" wide ribbon or ½" wide leather for the zipper pull (optional)

Photocopy and cut out the patterns on pages 136-137.

CUTTING THE EXTERIOR

1. Cut out the center area indicated on the Fussy Cut Guide (see page 136). Position the template over the Feature Print. Use the Exterior Inside Pleat template as well to ensure the full pattern piece will fit on the fabric and the desired portion of the Feature Print is going to be visible.

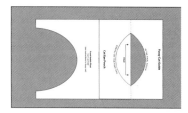

CAT-EYE ZIPPER POUCH

The Cat-Eye Zipper Pouch has a unique front curved pleat to perfectly frame that favorite fussy-cut or out-of-print fabric you've been hanging on to. When I was not sure what to name it, my husband said the shape looked like the center of a cat's eye, and the name stuck!

This pouch is an ideal size to make for a teenager to carry their jewelry or makeup in, or for your organized relative to keep their planner and pen protected from everything else in their purse. This pouch is fun to personalize for gift giving or to use in a #pouchswap. Frame a favorite character, design or even a hand-embroidered monogram in the center pleat.

2. Using a water soluble marker, trace around both templates, including the outer edge of the Fussy Cut Guide and the center fold. Fold the fabric in half along the center fold mark. Cut the Exterior Inside Pleat according to the template notations, aligning the marked line with the fold on the template. Do not remove the markings yet.

INTERFACING THE FABRIC

1. Fuse the Zipper Interfacing to the wrong side of each Zipper Side rectangle. The Interfacing rectangles will be smaller than the Exterior rectangles.

2. Fuse the Interfacing to the wrong side of the Exterior Back, setting the second Exterior Back Interfacing aside.

> **TIP:** *If you'd like more structure, add additional Interfacing to the Exterior Inside Pleat, Lining, and Exterior Sides. Trim all seam allowances ⅜" from the interfacing before fusing.*

ASSEMBLING THE EXTERIOR

This pattern uses a ⅜" seam allowance unless otherwise noted.

1. Position the Exterior Inside Pleat and Exterior Front right sides together, aligning the raw edges of the outer curve. Stitch around each of the curves, then trim the seam allowance to ⅛" using pinking shears.

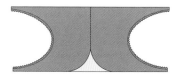

2. Turn the assembled unit from Step 1 right side out, pushing out the curves gently. Press well and edgestitch along the curves, beginning and ending ¾" away from each short edge.

3. Press the Pleat fabric right sides together along the two marked lines (these lines were the side markings from the fussy cut template). The Exterior edges will overlap, framing the fussy cut Feature Fabric.

45

4. Position the remaining Exterior Back Interfacing on the wrong side of the assembled unit from Step 3, aligning the raw edges. Fuse firmly with the pleat folded. Cross the Pleat ends and baste them in place using a ¼" seam allowance.

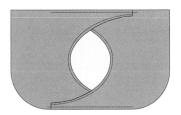

5. Position the assembled unit from Step 4 and the un-interfaced Zipper Side, right sides facing aligning the long raw edge. Stitch and press the seam

allowances toward the Zipper Side. Edgestitch along the seam, stitching on the Zipper Side.

6. Repeat Step 5 with the Exterior Back and remaining Zipper Side.

EXTERIOR BACK

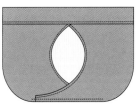

EXTERIOR FRONT

INSTALLING THE ZIPPER

1. Fold the Zipper Tab in half with the wrong sides and long edges together and edgestitch along the folded edge. Cut this piece in half to make 2 Zipper Tabs that are 1" x2" rectangles.

2. Follow the Signature Basic Bag instructions from page 8 for assembling the pouch. But omit the boxed corners and trim the curved edges of the Exterior and Lining panels before turning the bag right side out.

TIP: *Instead of using zipper tape, try using a regular school glue stick to baste these zipper Tabs in place.*

BY JESY ANDERSON

Finished Size: 9"

MATERIALS

Main Felt: 10" square

Contrasting Felt: 5" square

Perle #8 cotton (contrasting or matching)

Hand-sewing needle

Polyfill

Water soluble marker

CUTTING

From the Main Felt, cut:
(2) Tooth units using the pattern (see page 142)

From the Contrasting Felt, cut:
(1) Mouth using the pattern (see page 142)

MARKING

1. Using a water soluble marker, transfer the eyes and any other extras you would like to add from the patterns provided (see page 142). Be sure to enlarge them to the required size.

2. Mark the opening from the pattern to the 'face' of the Tooth.

> **TIP:** Feel free to disregard the eye shapes I have provided on page 142 and draw your own!

ASSEMBLING TOOTH FAIRY PILLOW

1. Using the embroidery floss and an embroidery needle, backstitch (see page 7) along the marked lines to stitch the Eyes onto the right side of a Tooth.

> **TIP:** Make it your own! Make the eyes stand out by using a metallic thread.

TOOTH FAIRY PILLOW

Who doesn't love the Tooth Fairy? Sometimes it's hard for her to get that tooth when it's under the pillow of a sleepy head though. So, the Tooth Fairy and I talked, and we came up with this pillow as an easy way for her to do her job efficiently! You can easily customize this to suit the child's preference in color or to match their room decor, and the sweet little embroidered smile is simply irresistible.

Consider cutting up all of the pieces of felt, gathering up some stuffing, embroidery floss and hand-sewing needles, pairing this with the Gift Bag on page 78 and gifting them the entire 'kit' for them to make one of their own! What better way to teach them some necessary hand-stitching skills? Creating this fun toothy pillow is fast and easy, use the enclosed template or increase the size to make a bigger pillow and adjust your felt sizes accordingly.

2. Position the Mouth approximately ¼" below the Eyes and centered on the Tooth. Using a blanket stitch (see page 7), attach the mouth in place sewing along the curved edge only.

3. With the wrong sides of the Main Tooth Felt units together and aligning the raw edges, stitch around the entire Tooth using a blanket stitch and leaving the 1" opening as previously marked to allow for the stuffing.

> **TIP:** Only use about 18" of thread at a time when hand stitching. Doing this prevents any knotting or tangled threads while stitching.

4. Stuff the pillow with polyfill until it feels firm but not so much that the stuffing is visible between the blanket stitches.

5. Close the opening from Step 3 using a couple of blanket stitches, knot and cut off the extra thread.

BY VICTORIA GERTENBACH

....

Finished Size: 3¼" H x 3¾" W

MATERIALS/CUTTING

For Fabric A, cut:
(1) 4½" square

For Fabrics B and C, cut:
(1) 2½" x 4½" rectangle

For the Patch Fabric, cut:
(1) 2" x 2½" rectangle
(1) 2" square

For the Lining Fabric, cut:
(2) 4½" squares

Pincushion filling

Water soluble marker

12 wt. cotton thread

Embroidery needle

Straight pins

NOTE: *The instructions given here are for creating one pincushion.*

ASSEMBLING THE PINCUSHION

1. Position the Fabric B and C rectangles right sides together. Stitch together along one long edge and press the seam open.

2. Position the assembled square from Step 1 on top of a Lining square, both right sides up and with the seam in the assembled square positioned horizontally. Place the Fabric A square on top and finally layer the remaining Lining square on top of Fabric A, both wrong sides up.

3. Pin to keep the four layers from shifting.

4. Machine stitch around the sides and bottom edge, making sure the seam on the assembled unit from Step 1 is still positioned horizontally.

PYRAMID PATCHWORK PINCUSHION

These fun shaped pyramid pincushions are the perfect project for using those assorted 5" squares of fabric from charm packs, or mixing and matching bits of leftover fabrics from your larger projects. I enjoy that they are simple to make, and great to give as gifts to your sewing friends! When choosing a filling/stuffing, I like to use something that will give the pincushion some weight so it stays put. My favorite filling material is ground English walnut shells, which can be found in pet stores. As a final touch, relax and have a little fun adding some decorative hand stitched patches and accents to your pincushions. I like to use 12 wt. cotton quilting threads in variegated colors that will complement the fabrics but also stand out, as the hand stitching helps make each pincushion extra special and unique.

NOTE: *Begin and end stitching by taking several backstitches to secure and prevent unraveling.*

5. Clip all four corners, being careful not to cut into the stitching.

6. Fold and press the top Lining and Fabric A seam allowances, wrong sides together. Turn over and repeat on the other side.

7. Position the assembled unit so that the pressed side seams from Step 6 nest together. Flatten the open edges together and pin in place. With a water soluble marker, measure in 1" away from each folded side and mark along the raw edge. Repeat on the other side. Sew up to the marks toward the middle of the assembled unit where the nested seams meet, leaving an opening for turning.

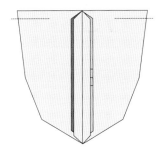

8. Turn right side out through the opening from Step 7 and use a blunt object, like a chopstick or similar, to gently push the points out. Fill with the filling.

> **FILLING TIP:** *Ground walnut shells used as a filler work great to give the pincushion weight as well as helping to keep your pins nice and sharp. However, they should not be used if tree nut allergies are a concern. You can use flaxseed, sand or dried rice mixed along with dried lavender, mint, chamomile, or crushed cloves to help repel unwanted pests.*

9. Fold the opening seam allowances inward with the wrong sides together. Stitch the pincushion closed using a whip-stitch and all-purpose thread.

10. Press in the edges of the 2" x 2½" Patch Fabric rectangle, by ¼" toward the wrong side.

11. Center the patch over the whipstitched seam from Step 9. Secure the patch in place using one or two straight pins. Hand-stitch the patch in place using the decorative 12 wt. cotton thread. Hide the beginning and ending knotted ends under the patch.

47

> **TIP:** *Creating irregularly placed stitches of similar but varying lengths can add some charm!*

12. Repeat Steps 10-11 with the remaining 2" square and position the patch anywhere you like on the Fabric A side of the pincushion.

13. Using the 12 wt. thread, add more decorative hand stitch-ing, covering all of the seams and add a few decorative large cross-stitches for extra interest.

48

BY SVETLANA SOTAK

. . . .

Finished Size: 4" x 3"

MATERIALS

Exterior: 10" square

Lining: 10" square

Medium weight fusible Interfacing: 1/8 yard

(1) 4" metal or nylon zipper

(1) 1¾" length of ⅜" – ½" wide Ribbon

Zipper foot

Optional: zipper pull and decorative tag

CUTTING

From the Interfacing, cut:
(2) 10" squares

NOTE: *Fuse the Interfacing to the wrong side of both 10" Exterior and Lining squares before cutting. The instructions given here are for creating one pouch.*

From the fused Exterior and Lining Fabrics, cut:
(1) 1" x 4¾" rectangle for the Top Panels
(1) 2½" x 4¾" rectangle for the Bottom Panels
(1) 3½" x 4¾" rectangle for the Back Panel

ASSEMBLING THE EXTERIOR

1. Referencing the Signature Basic Bag assembly on page 8 and omitting the zipper tabs, use the Exterior and Lining Top and Bottom Panels to attach the zipper. Your Front Panel should now measure 3½" x 4¾".

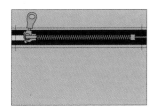

MINI COIN POUCH

This sweet pouch is perfect to keep spare change, credit cards, or your ID at hand. You don't need much fabric to whip up this little cutie so it's a perfect project to use up some leftover scraps of your favorite fabric.

Consider gifting this along with Anna's Wallet (see page 28) for someone you love who is just learning about managing money!

ASSEMBLING THE BACK PANEL

1. Position the Lining Back Panel and the assembled Front Panel with the right sides of the Linings together, aligning all the raw edges. Pin or clip to hold both panels together. Baste around the perimeter using a 1/8" seam allowance. Trim off any extra zipper tape.

2. Fold the Ribbon in half along the short side and position on the Exterior Bottom Panel, 1/8" under the left bottom zipper tape edge. Align the raw edges and baste in place using a 1/8" seam allowance.

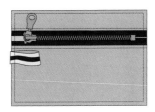

FINISHING

1. Position the assembled Front Panel and Exterior Back Panel, right sides together, aligning the raw edges. Pin around the perimeter and stitch around the entire Pouch leaving a 2¼" opening in the bottom seam for turning.

TIP: *Begin stitching about 1" from the left bottom corner and finish about 1" from the right bottom corner. Use caution when stitching to make sure your needle doesn't hit the zipper ends, especially if you are using a metal zipper!*

2. Clip the corners, being careful not to cut through the stitching. Press the seams open and turn the pouch right side out through the opening from Step 1. Push the corners out using a chopstick or similar blunt object to make them nice and pointy.

3. Hand stitch the opening in the bottom seam closed and give the pouch a good press.

OPTIONAL: *See page 11 for instructions on adding a zipper pull. Attach a decorative tag, vintage button, pretty bead or a favorite enamel pin if desired.*

BY NICOLE YOUNG

Finished Size: 20" x 23"

MATERIALS

Background: ¾ yard

Pocket: ¼ yard total

Thread Catcher: ¼ yard

Binding: ¼ yard

Batting: ¾ yard

(11–15) 10" x 1¼" Selvage Strips

¼ yard of fusible Fleece

½ yard of lightweight fusible Interfacing

2¼ yards of ⅜" wide trim

6" long strip of pom pom trim

(1) 1" button

1 sheet of 20# paper

CUTTING

From the Background Fabric, cut:
(2) 20" x 23" rectangles
(1) 20" x 5¼" rectangle
(1) 7½" x 3¼" rectangle
(1) 3" x 3¼" rectangle

From the Pocket Fabric, cut:
(2) 5¼" squares
(1) 3½" x 5¼" rectangle
(1) 3" x 5¼" rectangle
(1) 5" x 5¼" rectangle

From the Thread Catcher Fabric, cut
(4) 5¾" x 6¼" rectangles

From the Binding Fabric, cut:
(3) 2¼" x WOF strips
(1) 1¾" x 21" strip

From the Batting, cut:
(1) 20" x 23" rectangle

From the fusible Fleece, cut:
(1) 20" x 5¼" rectangle

From the fusible Interfacing, cut:
(1) 12" square
(2) 5¾" x 6¼" rectangles
(1) 7½" x 3¼" rectangle
(1) 3" x 3¼" rectangle

From the ⅜" wide Trim, cut:
(3) 5½" long strips
(1) 3" long strip
(4) 12" long strips

UNDERCOVER MAKER MAT

This dual purpose organizer converts from a useful mat under your machine to a sewing machine cover with side ties when not in use. As a mat, the double pockets and a removable thread catcher keep all your notions to hand and your workspace tidy. Share your pictures with #undercovermakermat!

ASSEMBLING THE MAT

1. Position a 20" x 23" Background rectangle wrong side up. Layer the Batting rectangle on top and the second 20" x 23" Background rectangle right side up. Pin and quilt as desired. Set aside.

> **NOTE:** If you plan on quilting heavily, cut the Background and Batting rectangles oversized, quilt and then trim to 20" x 23".

ASSEMBLING THE POCKET PANEL

1. If using the Butterfly Block (see page 128), photocopy the paper piecing pattern (see page 129) and assemble per the instruction. Trim the paper pieced block to 5" x 5¼".

2. The Pocket Panel is created by first piecing the main row of Pocket fabrics, then adding the secondary Selvage Pockets on top, using the Trim to hold everything in place. Arrange the Pocket pieces according to the illustration below. Sew together on the 5¼" sides and press. The panel should measure 20" x 5¼".

3. Fuse the Fleece to the wrong side of your assembled Panel from Step 2 and set aside.

> **TIP:** When selecting fabrics, keep in mind that the 2 left rectangles will be partially covered with the Pocket Front, as will the rectangle to the right of the Center Square. The far right square will be mostly covered by the Thread Catcher.

ASSEMBLING THE SELVAGE POCKETS

1. On the sheet of 20# copy paper, draw a 7½" x 3¼" and a 3" x 3¼" rectangle. Roughly cut them apart outside the drawn line leaving at least 1" around each rectangle.

2. Working with the larger rectangle first, draw a line from the top right to bottom left

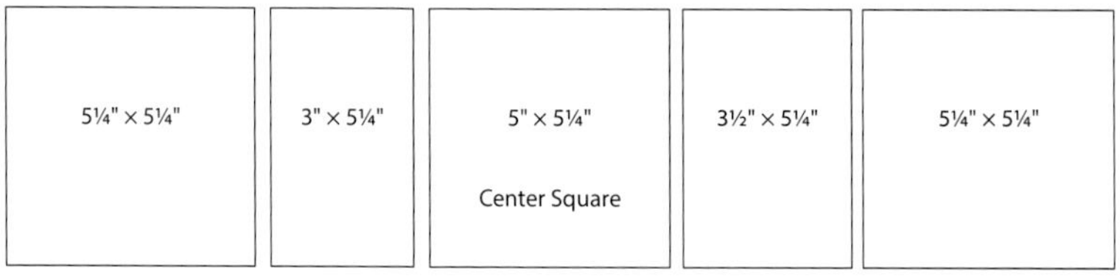

5¼" × 5¼"	3" × 5¼"	5" × 5¼" Center Square	3½" × 5¼"	5¼" × 5¼"

corner to use as a guide to establish the angle of the selvages. Positioning the selvages at an angle is a matter of preference. Feel free to position the Selvage Strips horizontally if desired.

3. Pin or glue a Selvage Strip along the bottom right corner, making sure the fabric extends beyond the drawn rectangle by at least ½". Stitch the selvage in place.

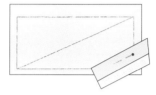

TIP: *There is a lot of room for improvisation when creating the Selvage Pocket Fronts. As long as the rectangles are fully covered, anything goes. Remember, selvage edges won't fray which adds a nice texture to the pockets, but feel free to use a single piece of fabric if desired. Get creative with your stitching too — I added one line of stitching to some Selvage Strips and two to some others.*

4. Position another Selvage Strip on top of the first, overlapping enough to catch both with the second stitch line, but showing a little bit of the fabric between (if desired). Top stitch in the same manner as you did with the first.

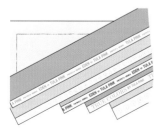

5. Repeat until the rectangle is entirely covered, then set aside.

6. Use the same method to attach Selvage Strips to the 3" x 3¼" rectangle. For variety, I positioned them horizontally rather than diagonally.

TIP: *For the 3" x 3¼" Pocket front, start with a piece of fabric at the bottom, rather than a selvage. This results in a cleaner edge since the Binding will overlap the bottom of the Pocket. Position the first piece covering about 2" of the bottom of the rectangle.*

7. Once both Selvage Pockets are pieced, position the rectangles with the wrong side facing up and trim along the drawn lines from Step 1. Carefully tear away the paper.

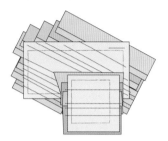

8. Fuse the 7½" x 3¼" rectangle of Interfacing to the back of the larger Selvage Pocket. Position the 7½" x 3¼" Background rectangle and the fused Selvage Pocket, right sides together. Sew across the 7½" edge. Position the assembled unit with the wrong sides together, press and edgestitch along the fold. Repeat with the two 3" x 3¼" rectangles, this time, sewing and edgestitching along the 3" edge.

9. Position the two assembled Selvage Pockets from Step 8 on the assembled Pocket Panel from Step 2 and baste across the bottom edge using a ⅛" seam allowance.

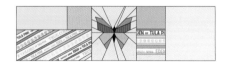

10. Position a 5½" length of Trim over each Selvage Pocket's vertical edges and pin or glue to hold in place.

TIP: *If you don't want to use trim, you can use additional Selvage Strips to cover the Pocket seams instead.*

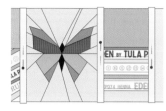

11. Edgestitch 2 lines vertically over each piece of trim. One line needs to catch your secondary Pockets and the second will just be decorative.

TIP: *I recommend checking your tension on a layer of equivalent thickness before stitching the Trim to your Pocket Panel.*

12. Because this is a straight line, save your fabric and use a simple 1¾" x 21" binding strip, cut on grain, to bind instead of a bias binding strip. Position the assembled Pocket Panel and the 20" x 5¼" Background rectangle, wrong sides together. Spray or pin baste to hold them in place. Align one raw edge of the Binding with the top edge of the Pocket Panel and stitch in the ditch of the first fold line.

13. Fold the binding over the top of the Pocket Panel enclosing all of the layers. Edgestitch along the bottom edge or hand stitch on the back, just as you would with a traditional quilt binding.

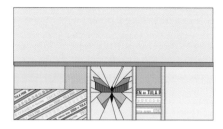

FINISHING

1. Position the completed Pocket Panel on the quilted mat, both right sides facing up and aligning the bottom and side raw edges. Baste around the two sides and bottom edge using a ⅛" seam allowance.

2. Using the Trim as a guide, stitch through all the layers from the bottom of the Pocket Panel up to the Binding, but not through it. Back stitch well at the sewing line nearest the Binding to keep the seams secure.

3. If not using the Machine Cover Option (following), use the remaining Binding strip and attach using your favorite binding method.

MACHINE COVER OPTION

If you want your mat to also be a sewing machine cover, use the following instructions for adding the ties before binding. If you simply want to use this as a sewing mat, use the Binding strips and bind using your favorite method and skip to the Thread Catcher instructions.

1. With the inside of the finished mat facing up, measure and mark the center of the left and right edges. Position the (4) 12" long Trim ties 4½" away from the center line with the length of the Trim positioned toward the center of the mat. Baste the short ends of the Trim in place along the raw edges using a ⅛" seam allowance and going over the Trim ends a few times to secure in place.

2. Using the (3) 2¼" x WOF Binding strips, attach the binding around the entire perimeter of the finished mat.

THE THREAD CATCHER

The Thread Catcher is designed to be removable with a small ribbon loop that hangs from a button sewn onto a Pocket Panel. My directions are for making the thread catcher as shown, but it can also be customized with any combination of fabrics, trims or patchwork.

1. Fuse the 5¾" x 6¼" rectangle of Interfacing to the wrong side of 2 Thread Catcher rectangles (one will be the Lining and one will be the Exterior Front). Mark and cut 1" squares off the left and right corners along the bottom 5¾" edge of all 4 rectangles.

2. To add the embellishments, position the 6" length of Pom pom Trim right side up, on the right side of a fused Exterior Front rectangle (or vertical placement if preferred) approximately ½" away from the un-notched 5¾" edge. Next, position a Selvage Strip right side down, upside down, on top of your Pom pom Trim and stitch along the bottom edge. Press the Selvage Strip down and edgestitch in the white Selvage space to secure them.

3. Fold an un-fused Thread Catcher rectangle in half, along the 5¾" edge. Finger press to find the center and create a crease. Position the 3" loop of Trim opposite the notched edge and center along the crease on the 5¾" edge. Baste in place using a ⅛" seam allowance.

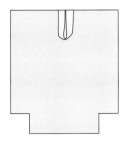

4. Position an un-fused and a fused Thread Catcher rectangle right sides together and stitch along the top edge. Press the seam open. Repeat with the remaining 2 Thread Catcher rectangles.

5. Position the assembled units from Step 4 right sides together. Pin to secure and stitch around the long edges and each short edge, leaving a 3" opening in one short edge for turning.

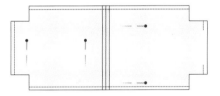

6. Box the corners using the Notched Method (see page 11).

7. Turn the Thread Catcher right side out through the opening from Step 5. Stitch the opening closed and fold the un-fused boxed rectangle inside the fused one to create the bucket. Press the top seam well and edgestitch around the top being sure that the Trim loop is positioned at the top for hanging.

8. Hand sew the button onto the far right block of the Pocket Panel. Loop the hanging trim on the Thread Catcher around the button and your Undercover Maker Mat is now complete!

BY NICOLE YOUNG

Finished Size: 5½" square

MATERIALS
A variety of scraps for the Wings
Black print scraps for the Body
⅛ yard of Background Fabric

ASSEMBLING THE BLOCK

1. Print the paper piecing pattern (facing) and piece together the 6 Sections using the paper piecing instructions on page 93.

2. After piecing two Sections together, remove your paper from the sewn seam allowance only and press the seams open and as flat as possible. This helps to reduce bulk and keep the overall size accurate. Repeat these steps each time you piece two sections.

3. Sew Section A to Section B, then add Section C onto this unit. Set aside.

4. Sew Section D to Section E, then add Section F onto this unit. Piece the top and bottom halves together.

5. Once all the Sections are sewn together, the block should measure 5½" square and is ready to be used as a 5" finished block. If the solid line on your paper pattern does not measure 5", trim your block from the right side using the center of the Body and the seam between top and bottom halves as guides. This seam falls slightly above center, 2⅜" down from the top when the block is trimmed to 5".

BUTTERFLY CHARM BLOCK

This little paper pieced block measures 5½" after piecing and can be used as a 5" finished square or trimmed to 5" for a 4½" finished square, making them perfect for mixing with 5" charms. The pattern has 6 sections that go together easily, but because the pieces are small, precision is key to ensuring that your sections line up. Be careful and accurate when trimming and always check your alignment before stitching.

This Butterfly is perfect for piecing into the Undercover Maker Mat (see page 124), but it can also be used as a centerpiece in the Pet's Mealtime Mat (see page 108), pieced into the front of the E-Reader Cover (see page 50), or into the exterior panel of the Knitting Bag (see page 106) or Passport Wallet (see page 70). This is scrap-friendly, so no materials are listed, but it will need about ⅛ yard of background fabric to complete.

BUTTERFLY CHARM BLOCK
(Actual Size)

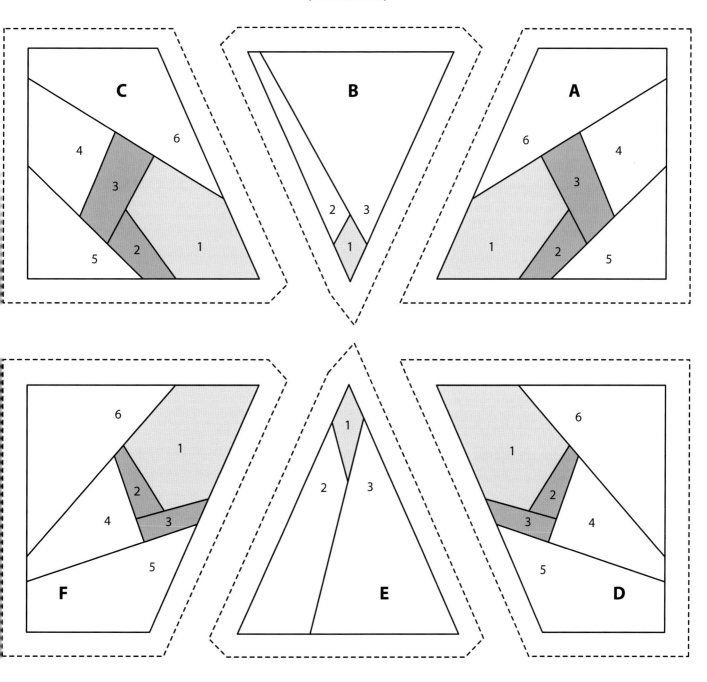

PATTERNS

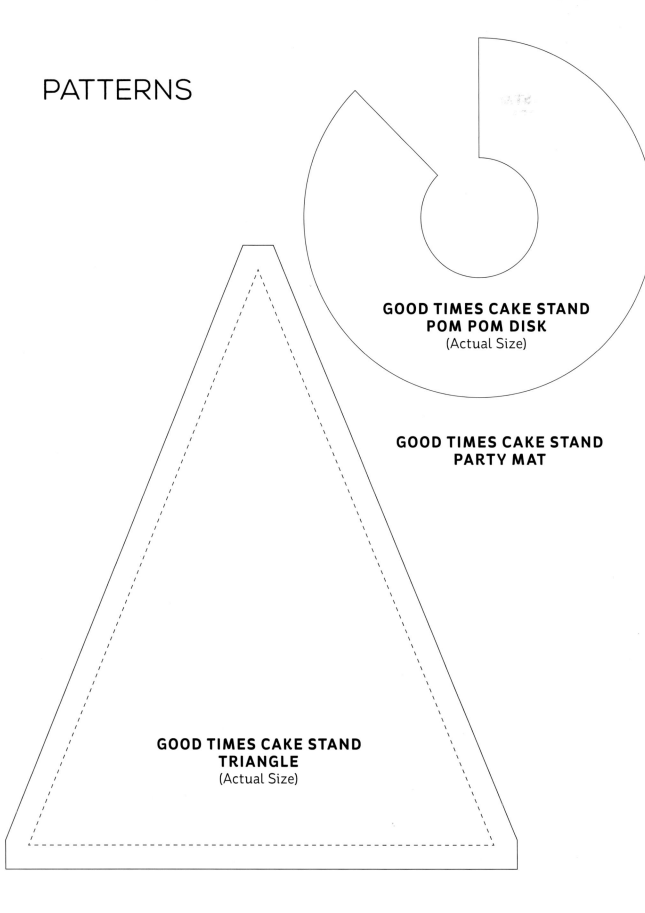

**GOOD TIMES CAKE STAND
POM POM DISK**
(Actual Size)

**GOOD TIMES CAKE STAND
PARTY MAT**

**GOOD TIMES CAKE STAND
TRIANGLE**
(Actual Size)

CHRISTMAS PICKLE ORNAMENT

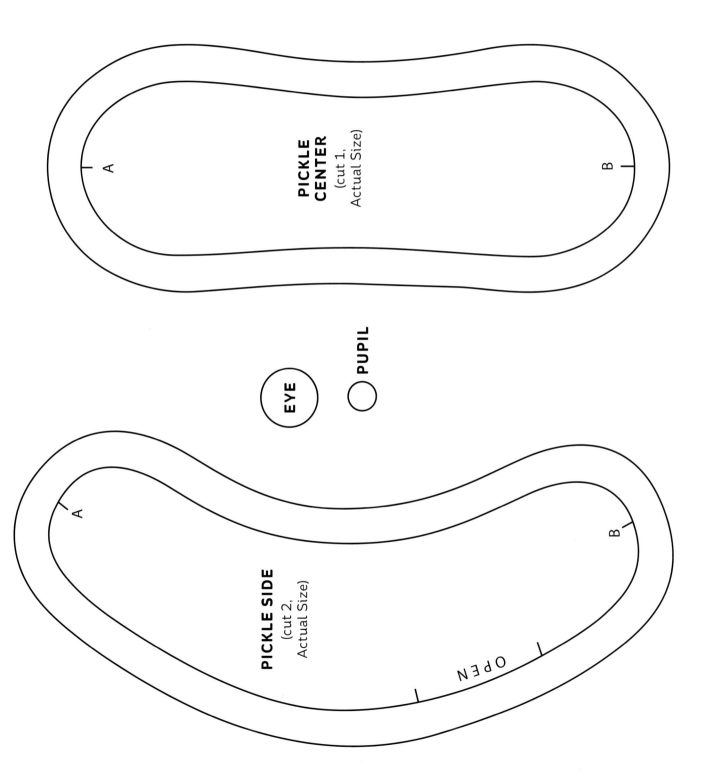

PICKLE CENTER
(cut 1, Actual Size)

A

B

EYE

PUPIL

PICKLE SIDE
(cut 2, Actual Size)

A

B

OPEN

DONUT POTHOLDER

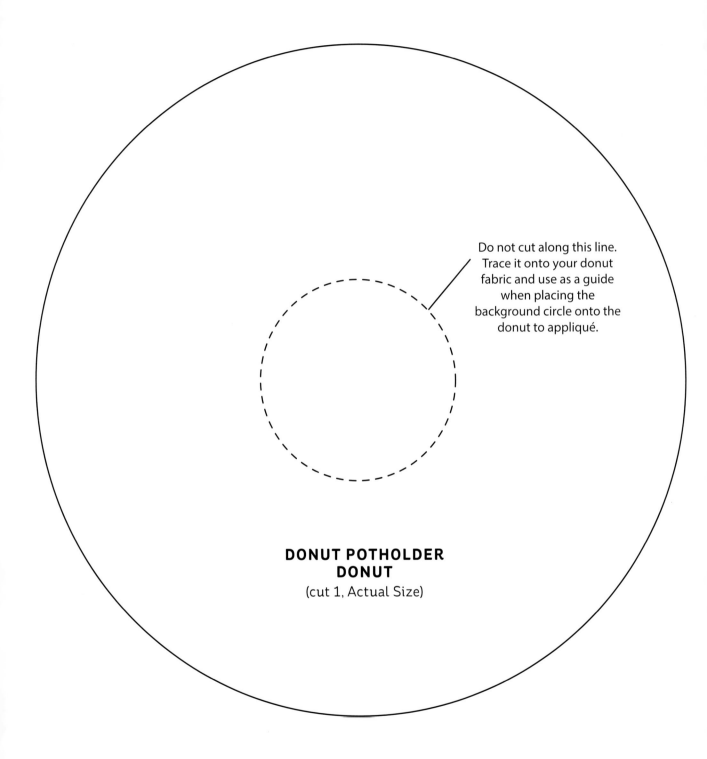

Do not cut along this line. Trace it onto your donut fabric and use as a guide when placing the background circle onto the donut to appliqué.

**DONUT POTHOLDER
DONUT**
(cut 1, Actual Size)

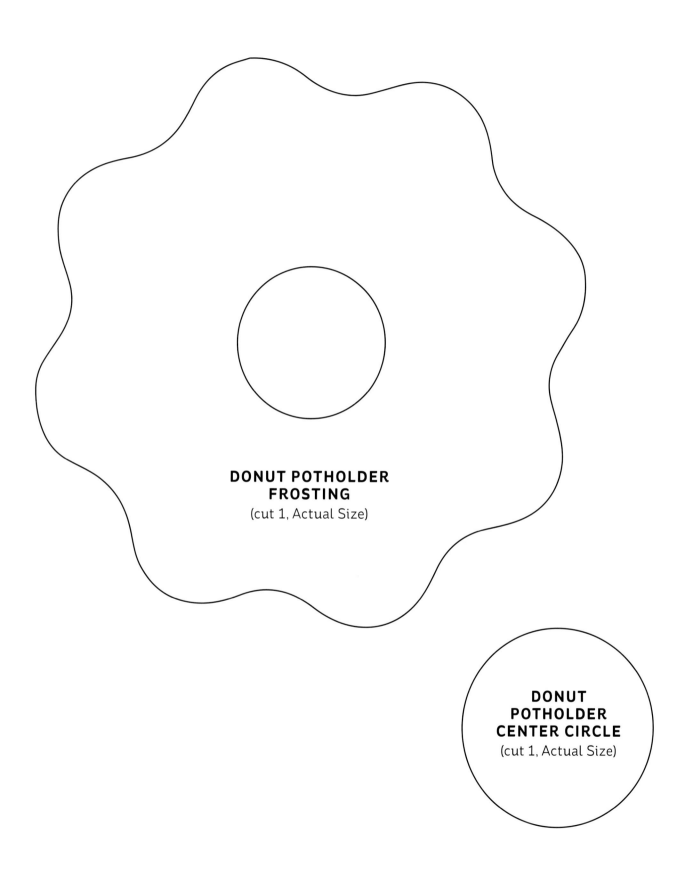

**DONUT POTHOLDER
FROSTING**
(cut 1, Actual Size)

**DONUT
POTHOLDER
CENTER CIRCLE**
(cut 1, Actual Size)

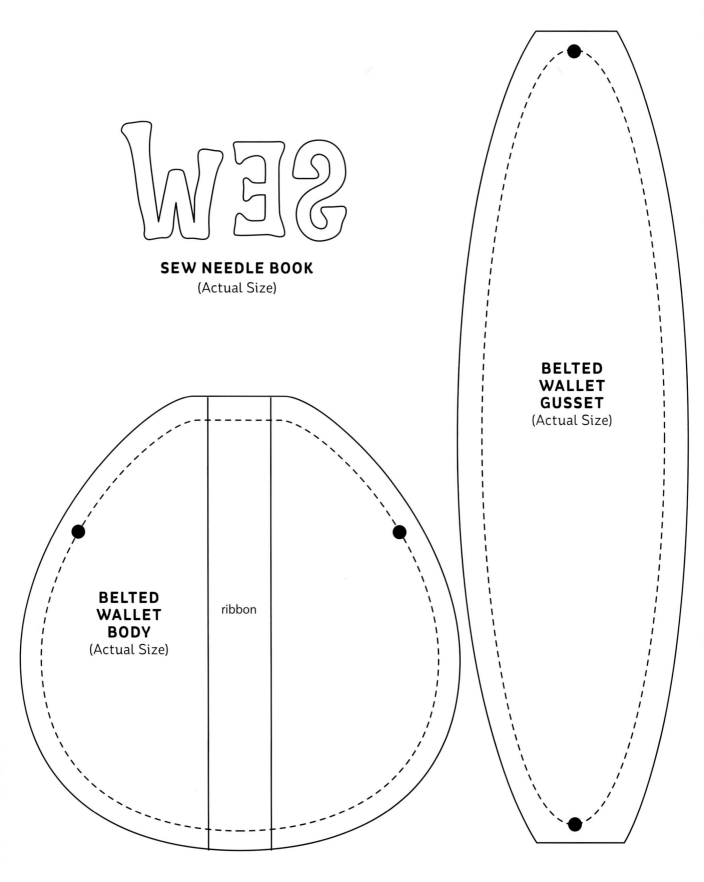

SEW NEEDLE BOOK
(Actual Size)

**BELTED
WALLET
GUSSET**
(Actual Size)

**BELTED
WALLET
BODY**
(Actual Size)

ribbon

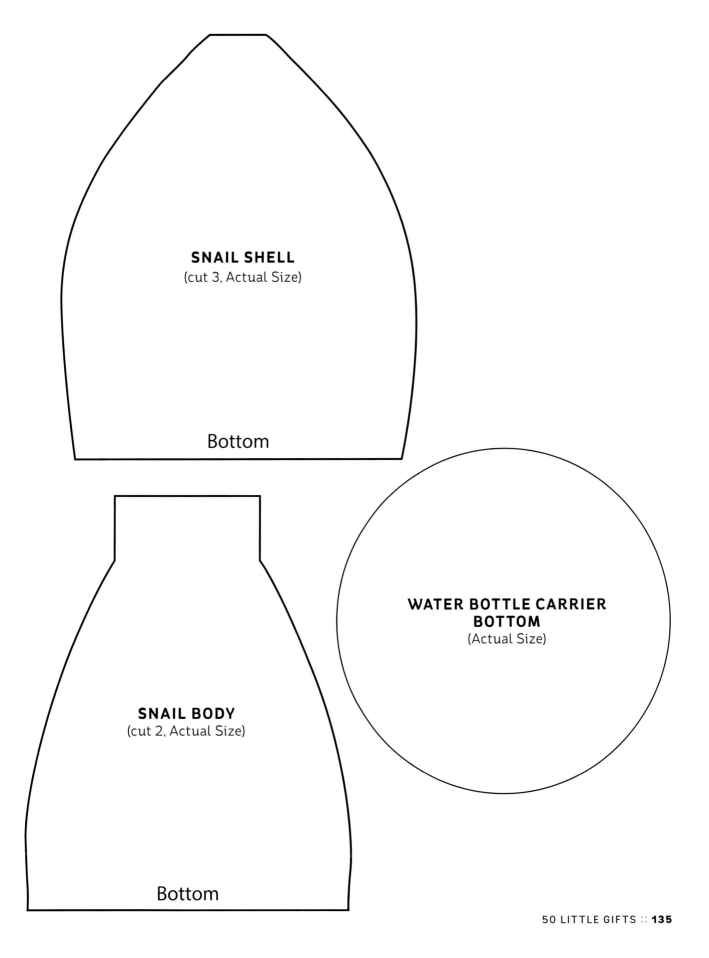

SNAIL SHELL
(cut 3, Actual Size)

Bottom

SNAIL BODY
(cut 2, Actual Size)

Bottom

WATER BOTTLE CARRIER BOTTOM
(Actual Size)

CAT-EYE POUCH
(Enlarge all Patterns 130%)

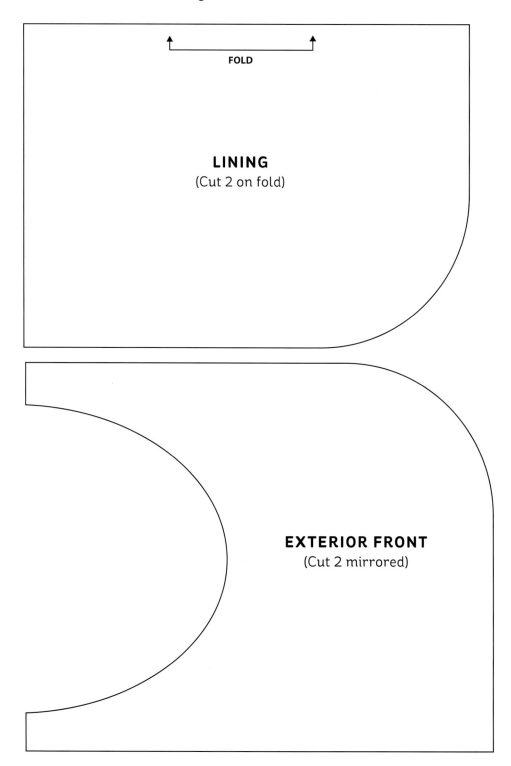

FOLD

LINING
(Cut 2 on fold)

EXTERIOR FRONT
(Cut 2 mirrored)

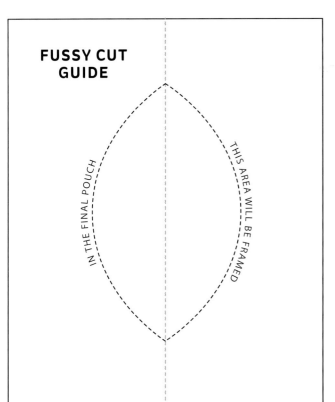

FUSSY CUT GUIDE

IN THE FINAL POUCH

THIS AREA WILL BE FRAMED

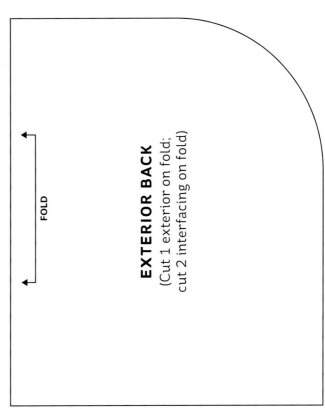

FOLD

EXTERIOR BACK

(Cut 1 exterior on fold; cut 2 interfacing on fold)

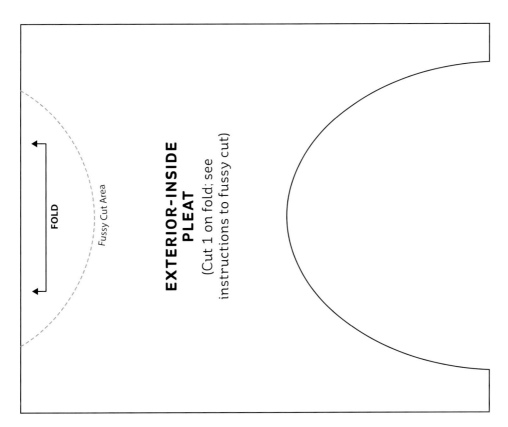

FOLD

Fussy Cut Area

EXTERIOR-INSIDE PLEAT

(Cut 1 on fold; see instructions to fussy cut)

ORANGE SLICE PINCUSHION

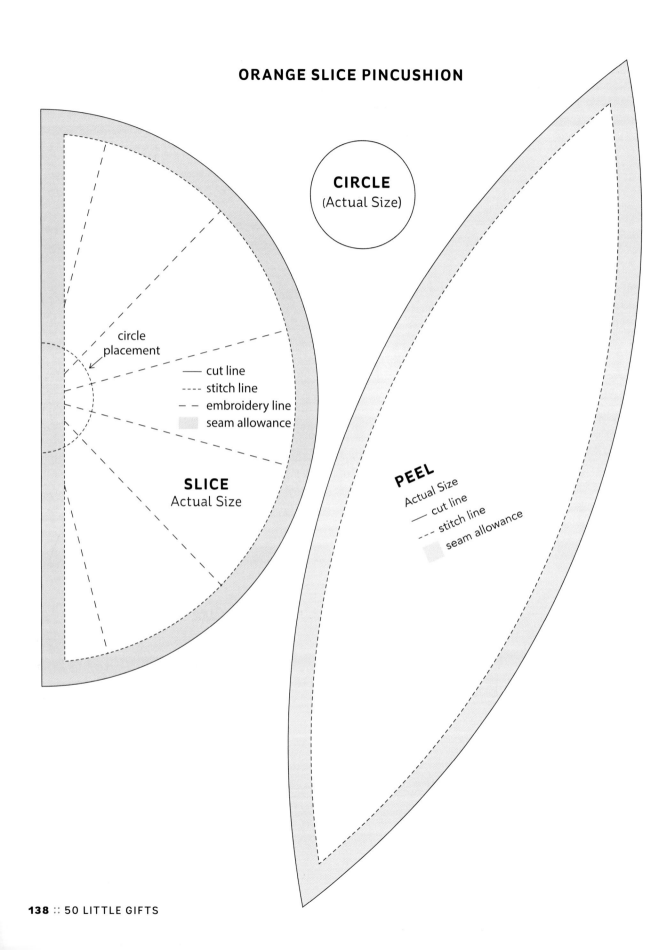

CIRCLE
(Actual Size)

circle
placement

— cut line
---- stitch line
-- embroidery line
▨ seam allowance

SLICE
Actual Size

PEEL
Actual Size
— cut line
--- stitch line
▨ seam allowance

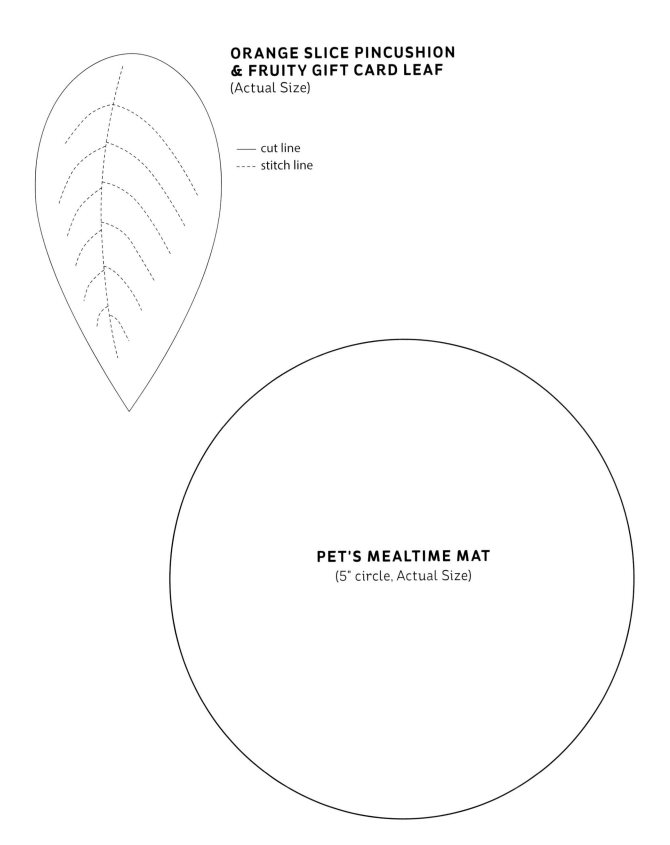

ORANGE SLICE PINCUSHION & FRUITY GIFT CARD LEAF
(Actual Size)

—— cut line

---- stitch line

PET'S MEALTIME MAT
(5" circle, Actual Size)

GEODE COASTER SET
(Actual Size)

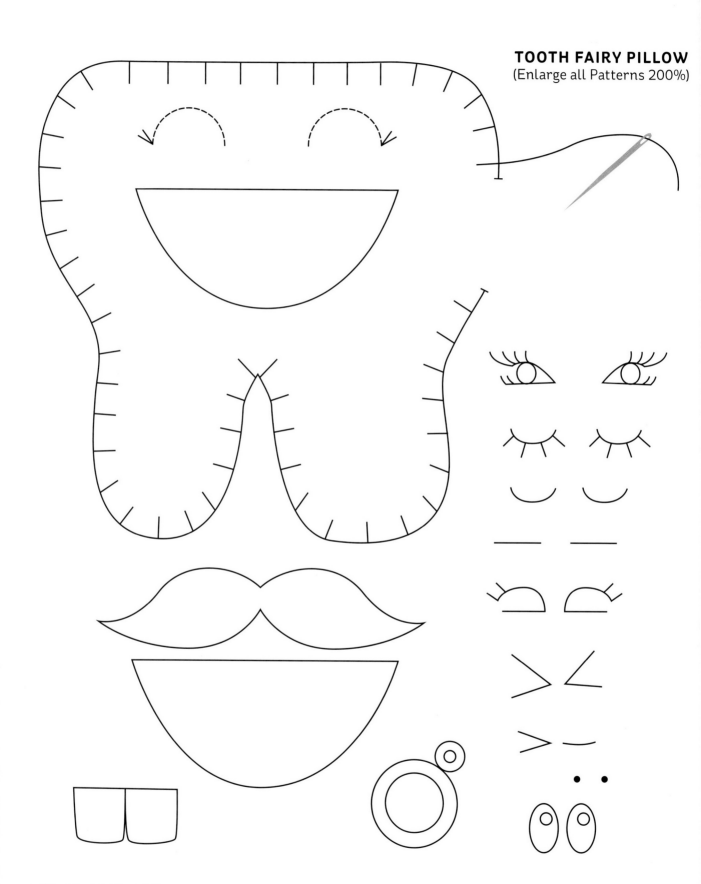

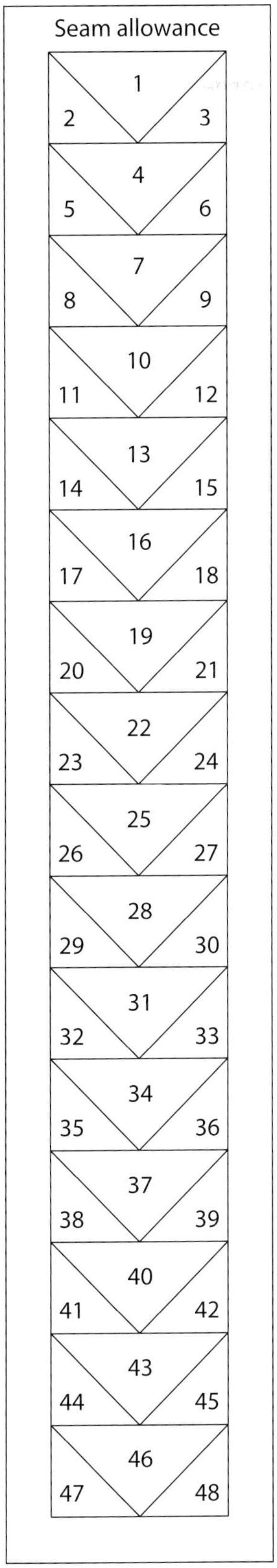

1
2   3
4
5   6
7
8   9
10
11   12
13
14   15
16
17   18
19
20   21
22
23   24
25
26   27
28
29   30
31
32   33
34
35   36
37
38   39
40
41   42
43
44   45
46
47   48

KEYCHAIN
(Actual Size)

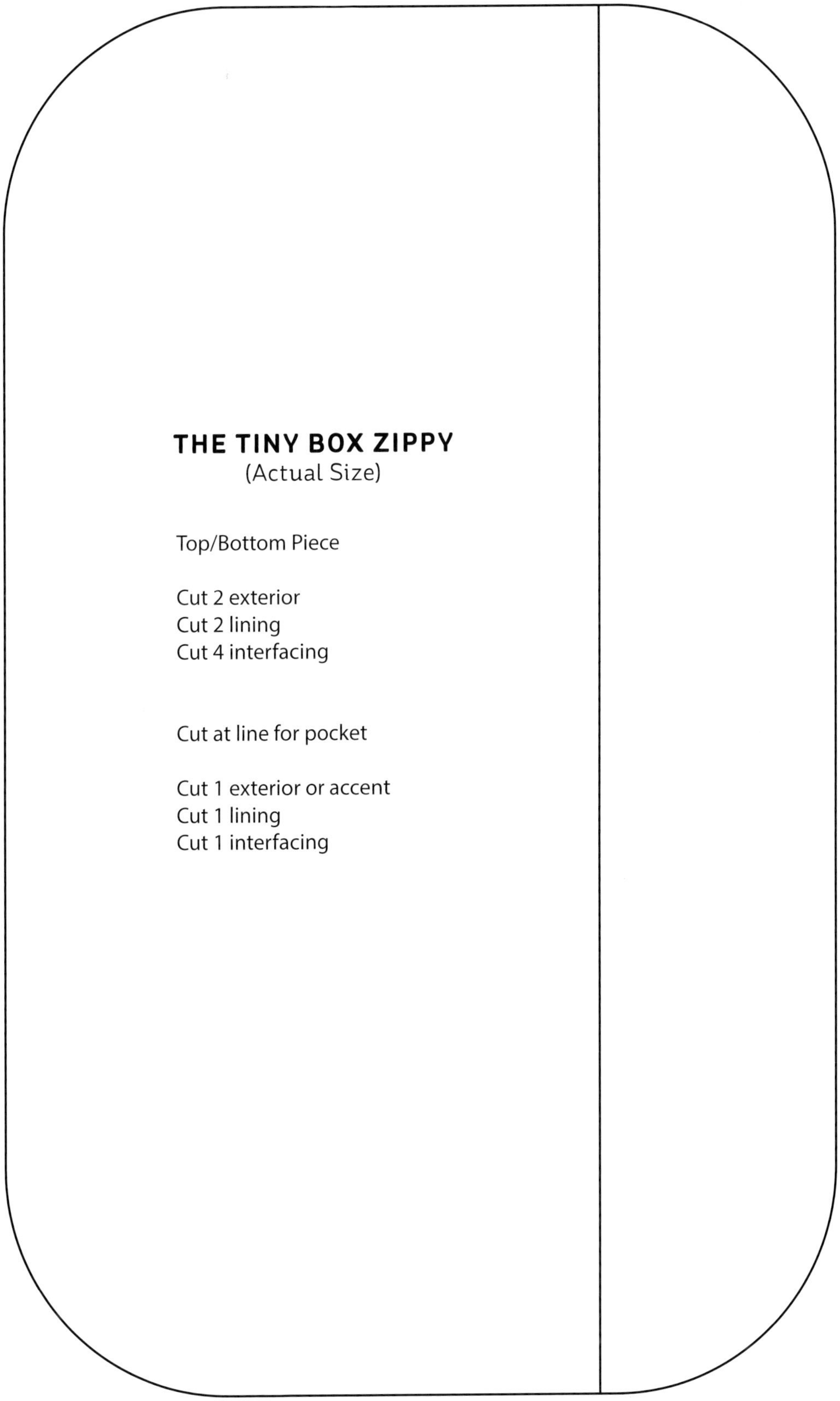

THE TINY BOX ZIPPY
(Actual Size)

Top/Bottom Piece

Cut 2 exterior
Cut 2 lining
Cut 4 interfacing

Cut at line for pocket

Cut 1 exterior or accent
Cut 1 lining
Cut 1 interfacing